It has been my honor to be involved with many of the ministries of OneHope and particularly to know Rob and Kim Hoskins. Kim is my niece, and for many years we have followed their life together and excitedly observed the way God has blessed them as they have worked with their family for this great cause.

I was on the ground floor in El Salvador for OneHope's first effort on a massive scale, when one million copies of the New Testament were distributed throughout that land. I saw personally the mobilization of hundreds of people who took the books in cars and sometimes horse wagons and mule backs to the most remote areas of El Salvador. I witnessed the tremendous reaction of children and even of their teachers as they received the Word of God with such gratitude. Some even stopped those messengers and asked, "Is this all you are going to do—give us this book? Please tell us more about Jesus." So we had that opportunity and privilege to do so.

This ministry has circled the globe and has had tremendous influence in our world today. The precious seed Jesus gave us to share with the world cannot be described in human terms, for it has blessing and influence and has the power to transform lives. I know this labor of love will affect destiny through the power of God's Word and will bless many. I highly recommend without any reservations the reading of *Hope Delivered* and the following of this fantastic ministry.

—JOHN BUENO
FORMER EXECUTIVE DIRECTOR, ASSEMBLIES
OF GOD WORLD MISSIONS

The Word of God has the power to change you. Rob Hoskins and the OneHope team live this out every day. Our church has been privileged to witness and partner with them in the eternal impact they are making in the individual lives of children around the world. This book is a must-read for anyone who wants to revolutionize their own life and the lives of others through the transforming power of God's Word.

—STOVALL WEEMS
ION CHURCH, JACKSONVILLE, FL
AUTHOR OF *AWAKENING*

D1369827

Rob's passion is contagious! I've known Rob Hoskins and his ministry, OneHope, for years, and he lives out what he writes!

I know of no other ministry that is bringing God's Word in such a unique and diverse way into every corner of the world.

The pages of this book are powerful. It's a must-read for every believer who wants to make a real difference in the world. You can influence others for Christ, and this book will show you how.

—JOE CHAMPION
LEAD PASTOR, CELEBRATION CHURCH, AUSTIN, TX
AUTHOR OF ROCKED

Leave it to the brilliant missiologist and futurist Rob Hoskins to put together an amazing book that combines the Word of God, children, destiny, and indomitable hope. The outcome is inspiration on every page and in every chapter. This is a great read and a manual for inspiring destiny and training leaders. Thank you, OneHope and Rob Hoskins, for making the world a better place. I continue to be one of your greatest fans!

—RON LEWIS
SENIOR PASTOR, MORNING STAR NEW YORK
SENIOR MINISTER, KING'S PARK INTERNATIONAL CHURCH,
RALEIGH/DURHAM, NC
COFOUNDER, CAMPUS HARVEST
FOUNDER, STRATEGIC CHINA INITIATIVE

Rob Hoskins believes there is more to life than most of us ever realize—that followers of Christ are intended to be "people of destiny" who affect the destiny of others. Rob has spent a lifetime traveling the world giving God's Word to children everywhere, and through this book of real-life stories he takes us on a journey to meet people of all ages whose lives have been transformed and whose destinies have been forever shaped. I commend Rob and recommend his book.

—MARK DeMOSS
PRESIDENT, THE DeMOSS GROUP
AUTHOR OF THE LITTLE RED BOOK OF WISDOM

Rob writes like he leads—with a missiologist's mind, a missionary's heart, and a pastor's touch. Hope Delivered is packed full of stories of lives changed by God's Word. If you want to know how to fulfill the Great Commission, read this book. Rob and OneHope don't just talk about changing the world…they're doing it!

—SCOTT WILSON
SENIOR PASTOR, THE OAKS FELLOWSHIP

OneHope has always been an organization of action, vision, and influence. They have literally traveled the world, spreading the gospel's reach through the Word of God. Through the lens of this amazing book Rob Hoskins allows us to travel with him to see and hear what the power of the Word of God does in the lives of people who, like you and me, are desperately in need of God's truth, hope, and healing.

—DINO RIZZO
LEAD PASTOR, HEALING PLACE CHURCH
AUTHOR OF SERVOLUTION

Wouldn't it be great if you actually discovered your purpose in life? Far too many people spend their entire lives wondering what they were put on the earth to accomplish. If you're not sure, then Rob Hoskins's new book, *Hope Delivered*, is the book for you. Read it. It will change everything about your future.

—PHIL COOKE
FILMMAKER, WRITER, AND AUTHOR OF ONE BIG THING:
DISCOVERING WHAT YOU WERE BORN TO DO

It is hard to read *Hope Delivered* and see what God is doing through the OneHope ministry without asking the question, "Am I doing all I can to give hope to a lost world?"

—DAVID GREEN
CEO/FOUNDER OF HOBBY LOBBY

Rob Hoskins folds his remarkable heritage and passionate spiritual calling into a clarion challenge to change the world!

—DAVID CRABTREE
LEAD PASTOR, CALVARY CHURCH, GREENSBORO, NC

In *Hope Delivered* my friend Rob Hoskins writes: "To know the future of a nation, you must know the state of its children." Around the world the state of children is desperate. In the developing world children suffer from abuse, disease, malnutrition, neglect, poverty, and violence. In the developed world they are offered an empty lifestyle of consumerism and no-rules sexuality. The Word of God is a book of hope that transforms lives and fills them with meaning and purpose. If you want to affect the destiny of the earth's children, then get the Word into their hands, heads, and hearts by all possible means! My prayer is that this book will inform you about the challenges children face today and inspire you to take hope-driven action on their behalf.

—Dr. George O. Wood
General Superintendant, Assemblies of God

HOPE DELIVERED

AFFECTING DESTINY

THROUGH *the* POWER

of GOD'S WORD

.

HOPE
DELIVERED

AFFECTING DESTINY

THROUGH *the* POWER

of GOD'S WORD

ROB HOSKINS

Most CHARISMA HOUSE BOOK GROUP products are available at special quantity discounts for bulk purchase for sales promotions, premiums, fund-raising, and educational needs. For details, write Charisma House Book Group, 600 Rinehart Road, Lake Mary, Florida 32746, or telephone (407) 333-0600.

HOPE DELIVERED by Rob Hoskins
Published by Passio
Charisma Media/Charisma House Book Group
600 Rinehart Road
Lake Mary, Florida 32746
www.charismahouse.com

Rob Hoskins has asked that all author royalties from the sale of this book be given to OneHope to bring God's Word to the children and youth around the world. For more information on OneHope, please visit www.onehope.net or call 1-800-448-2425.

Cover design by Studio Gearbox
Design Director: Bill Johnson

Visit the author's website at www.onehope.net.

Library of Congress Control Number: 2012910018
International Standard Book Number: 978-1-61638-675-7
E-book ISBN: 978-1-61638-676-4

First edition

12 13 14 15 16 — 9 8 7 6 5 4 3 2 1
Printed in the United States of America

This book is dedicated to the hundreds of thousands of
OneHope partners around the world who, through amazing
sacrifice, bold faith, and loving compassion, have delivered
hope to nearly a billion children and their families
around the world. You are my heroes!

CONTENTS

Foreword by Stovall Weems. xv

Introduction: A Wasted Life xvii

1 Heritage of the Miraculous 1

2 How Important Are They? 13

3 God's Word in a War Zone 25

4 Rob and Kim. 37

5 Once I Was Blind 47

6 Now I See. 57

7 The Silent Revolution. 69

8 So What? 81

9 Affect Destiny—What Does It Mean? 89

10 Seen and Unseen 101

11 A Better Mousetrap 113

12 Wake Up and Fight. 123

13 Spiritual Justice 133

14 And Justice for All 143

15 Cultivate Avondale 151

16 Choosing Life 163

17 Creative Spark. 173

Conclusion: Prescription for Success 183

Afterword by Bob Hoskins 191

Notes 195

FOREWORD

THE WORD OF God has the power to change you. If you're looking for evidence of this, you need to meet Rob Hoskins. Spend just a few minutes with Rob, and you'll know his life is not his own. His family, his ministry at OneHope, and his personal journey in serving God are proof of a life that has been radically transformed through the Word of God. It's the kind of life story that will inspire you and mess you up in the best sort of way. I will never forget how it changed my life and the life of our church.

Rob's heart for the next generation and those who are far from God is undeniable and contagious. Celebration Church was privileged to have Rob as a guest speaker at one of our Sunday church services. During his message Rob shared powerful stories of how God has used OneHope to bring the Word of God to children around the world and change their futures.

That Sunday Rob shared the story of how God gave his father, Bob Hoskins, the vision to start OneHope with a burden to bring the Word of God to every child in the world. El Salvador was the first country that contacted Bob to ask for Scriptures for every schoolchild in the country—968,000 children and youth. Through a miracle of rapid generosity, OneHope was able to provide God's Word to every school and every student in El Salvador. Teams of volunteers took the books to areas around the country, and many young lives and the lives of their parents were transformed through the gift of God's Word.

Toward the end of the service one of our staff members

approached me and shared a unique story about one of our faithful volunteers, Hilton, who had been listening to Rob's message. As Rob was sharing the story about El Salvador, tears started streaming down Hilton's face. Hilton was one of the 968,000 children who received a *Book of Hope* at school in El Salvador when he was a child. After receiving the *Book of Hope*, Hilton committed his life to Christ. Through the faith and obedience of Bob Hoskins and the OneHope team, Hilton's life was forever changed for eternity. On this Sunday—many years after first receiving the *Book of Hope*—Hilton had the opportunity to meet the son of the man who obeyed God's call to place the Word of God in the hands of children around the world. Rob had the chance to meet a spiritual brother.

Our church was wrecked after learning this story and inspired to reach "the one" for God. Personally, my passion to reach lost souls for Christ was renewed like never before. Since then our church has been proud to partner with OneHope in local and global initiatives to reach more people for Christ. Under the leadership of Rob Hoskins, OneHope is one of the most powerful and strategic ministries in the world bringing the Word of God into people's hands.

Hilton represents just one of many transformed lives. There are so many others around the world who have been touched by the Hoskins family and OneHope. They've found new purpose and identity in God and are changing the lives of others around them. You'll find their stories in *Hope Delivered*.

As you read through the pages of this book, I'm confident your own passion to reach lost souls for Christ will be stirred up like never before. How can the Word of God be used in your life? Perhaps you're searching for purpose or calling. You might simply be looking to renew your faith in God. Read *Hope Delivered*, and discover how God can use you to transform the lives of others. I promise your life will not be the same. In fact, it may change your destiny.

—STOVALL WEEMS
LEAD PASTOR, CELEBRATION CHURCH

Introduction

A WASTED LIFE

WHAT DO YOU hear when your cell phone rings? Right now, I hear Switchfoot's "Meant to Live."

Dreaming about Providence
And whether mice or men have second tries
Maybe we've been living with our eyes half open
Maybe we're bent and broken, broken
We want more than this world's got to offer…
And everything inside screams for second life, yeah.
We were meant to live for so much more.[1]

It's my firm belief—and all my life experiences and family heritage have clearly taught me—that we were meant to live for so much more! I know in my soul that followers of Christ are intended to be people of destiny who become agents of change for affecting the destiny of others. The ministry that I lead, OneHope, has this at its core. Our mission is: to affect destiny by providing God's eternal Word to all the children and youth of the world. The true stories I'll share with you in this book will show you just how powerful God's Word is to transform lives and shape destiny. I hope the book itself will give you ideas for how you, personally, can become the person of destiny God meant *you* to be.

Do you know who that is? Do you know who you are? Do you define yourself as a dad, a pastor, a mom, a lawyer, a chef, or a banker? Is that who you are, or is that what you do? This reminds me of the day I went to introduce myself to our new neighbor.

As is almost always the case when two American males meet, the inevitable question came up: "What do you do?" My ready answer is simple: "I give God's Word to kids around the world." Nothing prepared me for my new neighbor's reaction to that.

He was hostile. Why, he wanted to know, would I *waste my life* giving "Jesus books" to kids when the next generation around the world is suffering from the ravages of war, gang violence, addiction, starvation, AIDS and other diseases, lack of education, lack of clean drinking water, and child prostitution? If I wanted to help children, why wasn't I giving them food, building them schools, rescuing them from their abusers and enslavers? What earthly good did I think I could do by telling them about Jesus?

His angry words about the suffering of the world's children brought a hundred scenes to my mind, and it occurred to me that I had seen firsthand far more of the world's suffering than my neighbor ever had or would. I grew up in Lebanon in the 1970s. I had seen what war does to children. Our home was adjacent to a huge Palestinian refugee camp—I played with those boys. They were my friends. When the Israelis bombed that camp (on a pretty regular basis), it was friends of mine who were killed or who lost their mother or their arms. I saw how the conflict broke their hearts and warped their minds.

Yes, I know what war and suffering do to children. I had been in Swaziland, one of Africa's poorest nations, a nation the UN once predicted would literally go *extinct* because of the AIDS epidemic, when a little girl of eleven or twelve approached a grown man in our party and said, "For two dollars, you can have me." She was hungry and knew only one way to make money so she could buy food. Yes, I know what poverty does to children.

I arrived in Russia the day of the 2004 massacre at Beslan. At a back-to-school festival Islamic radicals had attacked and taken the students hostage. There was a horrifying three-day-long standoff as the frightened children were terrorized and denied food and water. When government forces attempted a rescue, bombs went off, and the children perished in fire and horror, along with their captors.

This was Russia's 9/11, but the *little ones* had been targeted. Russian men and women couldn't wrap their minds around it: Who would specifically set out to terrorize and *kill children?* I went to Beslan. I walked the bloody hallways of the decimated school and passed by the tombstones of children where parents and grandparents still lay prostrate on the ground, weeping with grief. I talked with heartbroken moms and dads, and traumatized and guilt-ridden siblings who survived. I know what violence does to children.

I didn't need my neighbor to lecture me about the suffering of children. I've seen that whatever ills befall a nation, community, or family, its worst effects are felt by those least able to combat them— the children. They're vulnerable, and they have no voice. What happens to them in their early years shapes their whole entire lives. I've seen how the enemy of our souls levels all the possible weapons of spiritual and physical warfare at them. He destroys children to create defective adults.

GOD'S WORD CHANGES DESTINIES

But here is what I also know, from my own personal experience and the myriad examples I've seen with my own eyes. The best possible thing we can do to alleviate the suffering of the world's children is to engage them with the gospel. The reason? Because the Word of God has miraculous power to transform.

Just as I understand far more acutely than my neighbor does about the global, systemic issues that face our planet's population, I also know that our most important commodity is not food, medicine, education, or any other material resource. Rather, it is hope. Without hope children, families, communities, and nations are destined for despair, pain, and destruction. And I know that the message of Jesus, found in the Word of God, is the only hope for the entire world. When His Word is discovered, engaged, and lived out—especially by children who hold the future in their hands and have a God-given disposition *toward* hope—it changes destinies.

This is why I do what I do. Of course, I know that we're all products of our heritage, which also explains much of why I do what I do. Our behavior is driven by our values, which are birthed out of our beliefs, which are formed by the stories we grew up hearing and believing. The story of my life began long before my birth—just as yours did. These stories are guiding, generational experiences and perceptions that build our reality. I'm going to tell you my stories, the stories that shaped my life, stories of the miraculous from before I was born and all along the way.

I don't know what your generational heritage has taught you. Maybe it was good; maybe it was bad—probably a mix of both. Here's what I *do* know, speaking as a preacher's kid whose heritage was a godly, missional heritage: the enemy of our souls seeks to marshal every lie that was ever told to us in our childhood and adolescence. He wants to use those lies to counteract any good and true story that our heritage was telling, and dictate a destiny of hopelessness. Thank God, Jesus Christ interrupts history and redirects destiny. In the next several chapters I'm inviting you to take a journey into my past and trace the power of Jesus Christ intersecting the generations before me to create my life and calling. You'll see the amazing destiny to which He's directing me, my wife, my children, and the generations to come—not just in my family but also all around the world.

As I said, I don't know your past, but I know Jesus Christ is ready and willing to affect your destiny and the destiny of your children or grandchildren, to use you (and them) to affect the destiny of that at-risk community on the other side of town or the remote tribes on the other side of the globe who are just waiting for the truth that will set them free and affect *their* destiny.

What do you say? Are you in? If yes, then this book will take you to the front lines of where a cosmic battle is being waged. It will show you living, miraculous stories of how the lives of children are being transformed and, by God's grace, how a global, spiritual revolution is building. It's a revolution that needs you as an active participant in affecting the destiny of our desperately needy world. I hope and pray you'll be part of it.

Chapter 1

HERITAGE OF THE MIRACULOUS

I T WAS A summer night in rural Oklahoma, and a husband and wife were driving home after a long night of partying. Charles and Lucille Hoskins—who would one day become my grandparents—didn't let the Great Depression get them down. My grandfather Charles had developed skill in making moonshine whiskey. He maintained a still in a cornfield to help support his mother and siblings during the worst days of the depression. As things began to get better, he had taken a job in the lab at the Continental Oil Refinery and married his childhood sweetheart, my grandmother Lucille. They both loved dancing and enjoyed partying as well. Much of their time during their courtship and after their marriage was spent going to dances and living it up into the wee morning hours. On this particular night as they were driving home late, they saw bright lights shining from a big tent in a field. Could it be another party? Curious, they drove out into the field toward the lights and stumbled into the unlikeliest place imaginable for them: an old-fashioned tent revival.

This, my friend, is how God *affects destiny*. This is how He affected *my* destiny. Breathe it in...imagine the scene...

Someone is preaching God's Word. Someone is leading in a chorus of "I Surrender All." Someone is praying for sinners to come home to Jesus. And somehow the Spirit of God slips past all their defenses to bring the party-loving pair into the light of Jesus Christ.

That's why my dad was raised in a Christian home. His parents became faithful church members, totally dedicated to the Lord, true believers in the life-transforming power of the Word of God. But I don't think they were prepared for the bewildering turn their life would take just a few years later when my dad was seven years old. During a church prayer meeting little Bobby Hoskins was transported in the Holy Spirit into the heavenly realms. For hours he lay before the altar while he received an extraordinary vision from the Lord.

At the culmination of this vision he found himself walking hand in hand with the Savior, against a great, oncoming tide of humanity. People all around him were walking past him and Jesus, unconscious of the presence of the Almighty, streaming toward a steep cliff, and walking off the end of it into the fiery abyss of hell. My father remembers, in the vision, that he cried out to those who were passing by him and Jesus; he tried to get their attention, to introduce them to the Savior, but they didn't seem to hear him. They just kept walking straight over the edge and into eternal damnation.

When the vision ended and my dad returned to consciousness, he had received his lifelong calling. He knew that he was commissioned to preach the gospel and lead sinners to repentance. He was seven years old, but he emphatically *knew* God had called him to preach from the pulpit not just to children but to adults. He told his parents that God wanted him to start preaching right away and carry the good news all across the United States.

Put yourself in my grandfather's shoes. Better yet, imagine the hardest-partying friend you have, the one least likely to come to church. Imagine that by some miraculous event he *does* come to know Jesus. Then a few years later his little boy declares God has called him to start preaching, and he wants his dad to take him all across the country so he can follow the calling. Most parents, I think, would have been happy their son was called to be a preacher and counseled him to keep walking with Jesus, finish school, go on to Bible school, get ordained, and then start his ministry. *Little boys aren't preachers, son. Little boys go to school.*

But my grandfather wasn't like most parents. He had an amazing faith, and he believed in the vision. I think the faith of my grandfather and his obedience to God's direction was truly astounding. He took Bobby to the pastor, had him explain his vision and calling, and asked whether the little seven-year-old boy could preach the following Wednesday. The pastor said yes! This was the beginning of my dad's ministry life. He was under the anointing from that very first message, hoping to bring people to new life in Christ. Signs and wonders followed. Gramps began traveling with my dad, who became known as Little Bobby, setting up speaking engagements for him and homeschooling him before there was such a thing as homeschool. He grew up on the evangelistic field, sharing the gospel of Jesus Christ night after night all across the continental United States from the time he was seven. The phenomenon of a child—who spoke with the vocabulary and maturity of an adult—attracted large audiences across America.

Ten years flew by, and my dad was called to the mission field. As a seventeen-year-old he went to British Guyana with $5.68 in his pocket and a one-way ticket. By faith he'd had contacts in Guyana rent a hall for a revival and do advertising and promotions—so he arrived in the country, a seventeen-year-old with next to no money, already several thousand dollars in debt for the arrangements that had been made, but he knew God had called him there to affect the destiny of this needy nation.

He began preaching, and by God's power people began to be saved and healed, and crowds began to pour in. The new believers learned how to be generous givers, and they more than paid for the rental of the hall and the promotional materials that had been done. In fact, they helped to finance my dad to go to several other nations of South America and share the good news. He spent three months on the mission field, introduced thousands to Jesus, and arrived home in the United States with five dollars in his pocket. His entire South American mission had cost him a whopping sixty-eight cents.

Every family has its own heritage: the grandparents who arrived in the United States through Ellis Island and launched their own successful business, the patriarch who served under Ulysses S. Grant in the War Between the States, or the younger son who fled to Mexico after that unfortunate incident with the cattle rustlers. The stories I grew up with were ones of miracles—how my grandparents came to know Jesus, how my dad became a child evangelist.

It was a somewhat similar story on my mother's side too. Her mom, my grandma, was Helen Eddy. Her father was a Canadian lumber baron who had seven profitable lumber mills, and he'd been preparing Helen to join him in the family business. He even sent her to university at a time when very few women went to college. Her life seemed destined to go in a particular direction as a savvy—and rich—businesswoman. But then God intervened and affected *her* destiny. Helen had an encounter with the Holy Spirit, joined a Pentecostal church, and started a preaching ministry of her own. Her mother was also a Spirit-filled believer and used her money and influence to bring a Pentecostal preacher, Clifford Crabtree, to town for some revival meetings. Helen met Clifford, and the rest was family history—they fell in love and planned to marry.

But Helen's dad, who would be my great-grandfather, was scandalized. He'd already been heartily embarrassed by Helen's joining the Pentecostals, those "Holy Rollers" from the wrong side of the tracks. He owned one of the first Model-A Fords in Canada, and he'd passed by his daughter on the street-corner preaching one day and actually yanked down the car's window shades so he didn't have to look at her making a fool of herself (as he viewed it). When he found out she was going to marry a Pentecostal preacher and make a life of ministry rather than coming to work with him, he was livid— and he disowned her.

She gave up status, money, and a career in business at a time when few women even worked outside the home—all for the sake of the gospel. And what Helen and Clifford did for the kingdom of God—it also became the stuff of family legend. They launched churches in Grand Manan, Prince Edward Island, and Halifax—some of the most challenging regions of Canada. They reared two boys and two girls (one my mom) and lost one baby girl to sudden infant death syndrome.

Another part of our family heritage is the irony that my grandma actually passed away on the same day that Howard Hughes died. The titan of industry who had devoted his life to making money died as a paranoid recluse; eight people attended his funeral. My grandmother, who gave up a fortune and a business career to follow God's call, had a funeral packed with hundreds of friends, as well as people she had helped lead to the Lord from everywhere she and my granddad had ministered.

I remember my mom's story about the funeral, how one of the speakers, Rev. Bob Gass, from Ireland, said that one of the greatest joys of growing up in Belfast had been following the lamplighter on his rounds. "We didn't always know where the lamplighter was, but we could tell where he had been," Bob said. "We can look across this congregation and know where Helen Crabtree, the lamplighter, has been."

I, of course, could see where she had been too because of the lives of my mother and her two siblings. Both Charles and David Crabtree became ministers, her sister an educator, and my mom—a talented musician and minister in her own right—married my dad and became his partner in a lifetime of global missions.

This was the heritage of the miraculous, the missional family heritage, in which I grew up. And then, of course, I grew up with Bible stories, particularly those stories of how God uses young people as agents of change, as mighty warriors and heroes. My dad understood this instinctively from his own experience, and he never failed to impress it upon my brother, sister, and me.

The Bible is replete with examples of the importance of children, the way God loves them and uses them. You see, children are born with hope. It's only time, experiences, and the relentless pressures of life under Satan's dominion that robs them of their God-given destiny.

- Samuel was called to God's service when he was but a small boy serving the priests.

- The anointing on David's life began when he was just a shepherd boy, and as a youth he killed the giant Goliath.

- Josiah was the "boy king" of Israel.

- Jeremiah claims in Jeremiah 1 that he was a mere child when God called him to be a prophet.

- Naaman's servant girl, a young Israelite, was instrumental in his seeking God's touch.

- Moses was chosen as the savior of his people when he was just a baby.

- Jesus Himself was only twelve when He astounded the elders in the temple, who listened to Him with respect, awe, intrigue, and wonder.

These were the stories that were instilled in me, when I was a boy, that children are important to our heavenly Father. God sees the intrinsic value and worth of children. He knows they have much to contribute to the church and ultimately to His kingdom. I've seen this truth demonstrated again and again throughout my entire life and ministry.

MURIEL

I think of one little girl who was instrumental in bringing her family to Christ. Muriel was a little seven-year-old Haitian child. Even before the devastating earthquake of 2010 Haiti had been a severely blighted nation. It was the poorest in the Western Hemisphere. It has a history of bloodshed, violence, and voodoo. In 2008, in one of the more "minor" horrible misfortunes that seemed to pummel Haiti regularly, a school collapsed. More than ninety children were killed, including Muriel's five-year-old brother. Muriel survived, but only because someone rescued her from beneath a pile of rubble and several corpses of her friends. Her legs were crushed, and the doctors came very close to amputating them. They managed to save them, but Muriel was crippled.

Her parents too were crippled, but in another way. They were heartbroken over the loss of their son, and they were consumed with anger toward God. When a team from the local church came to comfort families in the community, Muriel's parents angrily rejected all they had to say. They had no use for a God who would take their son away. Muriel, though, was more willing to listen and very happy to receive her *Book of Hope* Scripture book. She soon chose to follow Christ as Savior. Although her parents were antagonistic to the gospel, Muriel quickly became very devoted to Jesus and her church.

Our OneHope ministry partners were able to connect her family with a medical mission so that Muriel received therapy and was actually able to walk again and could return to school in fall 2009.

Then came the massive 2010 earthquake. Muriel's mom was out shopping. Muriel was home with a tutor who was helping her catch up in school. Their neighborhood was in the area hardest hit, and Muriel was killed.

A few weeks later our partners returned to the area to offer comfort and hope to families that had once again been decimated. They dreaded the reception they would get from Muriel's parents—after losing their little boy three years before and now their daughter.

Muriel's father was still in the neighborhood, but he had sent his wife away to relatives. She was expecting another child, and he wanted to protect her as much as he could from the stress of the quake's aftermath. Surprisingly, he did not reject the words of the church team when they came to visit him. In fact, he said he wanted to be sure that he would see his Muriel again in the life to come, and he prayed with them to accept Christ as Savior! Muriel's example of commitment had been a witness of God's power to him.

Weeks later his wife returned. She had lost the baby.

Our partners feared this new setback would throw the family once again into despair and turmoil. But in fact, Muriel's mother had also committed her life to Christ, and the couple is standing strong in their faith, despite their grief. In her life and her death Muriel was a missionary to the people she loved best. Because of her choice to follow Jesus, her parents have also committed their very lives to Christ, and they know they will one day be reunited with her.

GIVE THE NEXT GENERATION A GODLY HERITAGE

The heavenly Father knows the power of a child's life. He loves the little ones for themselves, and He allows them to become creative agents of change for their families and communities when they share His love. My own father, as a child and teenager empowered by the Holy Spirit, brought thousands of people to new life in Christ, and of course, thousands *more* through his continuing ministry as an adult.

I have a family heritage of the miraculous. It's a heritage I've been privileged to share with my own two daughters. If you're a parent or a grandparent, I encourage you to give your children the amazing gift of their own godly heritage. Reach out in your own neighborhood and community—and even around the world—to the "spiritual orphans" who have been denied this heritage. You can help to give it to them, by sharing the good news and by affecting their eternal destiny with the touch of God's love. I hope, in reading my story and discovering the ministry of OneHope, you'll come to understand just how critical this is for our own Christian families and for the millions who have yet to receive a relevant presentation of the gospel.

I've been impressed with the writings of Harvard psychiatrist Robert Coles, who has written books such as *The Moral Intelligence of Children* and *The Spiritual Life of Children*. It's his contention that historically children had an immediate grasp of their place in the world and their purpose in life because they understood the output of their parents. In an agrarian society children were part of the work on a family farm, and they knew that what their dad did was feed the community by growing crops or by cattle ranching—in fact, not only did they know that this was what Dad did, but they also knew they were part of it. Then during the Industrial Revolution, as manufacturing came into its own, America's children weren't directly involved with the work product of their parents, but they understood it: *my dad makes railroad cars* or *my dad makes iron hammers.*

Today parents go to offices, and children really have little to no idea what they do there. Nothing tangible is produced by the work of the parents for children to see. Coles believes children have lost their identity because they don't know what their parents do or what difference their parents' work makes in the world. All they know about their parents' careers is that their parents are "gone to work" the majority of their childhood. I didn't want this for my daughters. I wanted them to know and understand what our lives were all about, just as I had learned it by being on the mission field with my parents. My wife, Kim, is a dedicated, godly mom, and as I pursued my global mission, she was always there for the girls, instilling God's unchanging truth in their hearts and minds.

They were good girls, they had good friends, but all the same, even as Kim and I presented them with a countercultural message of the radical love of Jesus Christ, the culture of twenty-first-century America was seeping into their thoughts and beliefs. This point was driven home to me dramatically the day I picked up my eldest and her friends from the mall. The backseat full of thirteen-year-old girls was buzzing with conversation about the G-strings they had just purchased. I thought, "These are the *nice girls*. This just isn't right."

Kim and I made the decision then not to let the culture shape our daughters but to show them how to form their lives through their godly family heritage. Each of my girls spent the year she was thirteen traveling with me and working on the mission field. I can't tell you what an impact this made on their lives. You won't find two young ladies more dedicated to the cause of Jesus Christ, more motivated by His love, and less influenced by the godless subculture of their generation.

The Jewish people still see year thirteen as the time when a child becomes an adult: a boy becomes a man, a girl becomes a woman. I know from my experience with my own children how true this really is and how pivotal this time was in the development of my girls.

Diandra, the eldest, spent a semester with missionaries in Benin, West Africa. It was incredibly difficult for me to send her there, incredibly difficult for her to adjust to her life in the third world without her friends back home and her support system. But when it was time for her to come home, she honestly didn't want to leave the bush and her ministry there. That experience showed her the enormous dichotomy between how most of the impoverished world lives, in squalor and utter hopelessness, and the Disney-esque world we've created for our children here in the West. It birthed in her heart a passion for spiritual justice, and she's pursuing this missional calling today as a grown woman.

Our younger daughter, Natasha, traveled with me and saw me doing my job every day and also spent a summer in Rwanda, a nation still dealing with recovery and reconciliation after a horrifying genocidal slaughter between the two tribes that make up most of the population. These experiences have formed a strong, steadfast heart in my little girl. She knows what she believes, and she speaks her mind. She understands her history, her heritage of the miraculous, and her family calling to share the Word of God with all who so desperately need to receive it.

I believe this is a gift we can give the next generation, even if their own parents and grandparents have failed to give it to them. Certainly it is a gift all believers ought to be giving to their children—a foundational knowledge of who we are and what we do as followers of Jesus Christ. Even if you never knew your parents or you know that your family has a heritage of behaving badly and getting things wrong, you can still decide that the *godly* heritage of yourself and your house begins right now. You can be the turning point for your family. I believe three generations down the road, you'll be the Charles and Lucille or the Helen and Clifford that your great-grandchildren look back upon and bless for changing their history and their destiny.

Chapter 2

HOW IMPORTANT ARE THEY?

HEROES, MINISTERS, AND agents of change—I told you the Bible provides multiple stories of *children* who were all those things. Why, my own dad was all those things as a child. I know God sees children as incredibly important.

But if you want a modern, secular answer to that question—How important are children?—I suggest you go to a marketing conference for the Fortune 500. One of our partners paid for me to attend. I was mesmerized. These men and women were insistent that in order to make your brand successful, you have to make sure it's ingrained in children by the time they're eight years old. Not just children's brands such as Coco Puffs or Power Rangers but *any brand.* To make sure your product sells to adults fifteen years from now, you have to instill it in children *right now.*

How do you do that? They suggested eight principles. Among the tools they recommended you can use to capture the minds of children eight years and younger are:

- Tribalism

- Rebellion

- Sexuality

I was stunned. As the list went on, I asked, "Is anyone else here at all concerned we're talking about getting into children's minds with rebellion and sexuality with no reference to character, ethics, or values?" My question wasn't answered. I was resoundingly ignored. There was no room for morality in the cutthroat world of marketing, just as there is little room for childhood in the dog-eat-dog world of the free market. Bottom line: branding a product in the mind of a child equals a consumer for life. That's what matters most.

The same principles apply in the spiritual world. For years it was believed in the American church, on anecdotal evidence, that 80 percent of adult Christians said they had made their decision for Christ prior to age eighteen. This, at least, motivated American believers to try to present the gospel to children, apparently the most fertile mission field, the most likely to respond. What we have discovered today is that the critical age window for reaching children and youth with the gospel has narrowed considerably: it isn't under age eighteen, but under age fourteen, when children need to be presented with the salvation message. The 4/14 Movement concluded that some 85 percent of America's believers chose Christ when they were between the ages of four and fourteen.[1] Today's teenagers over that age, in the fourteen to eighteen segment, are actually least likely to respond to the claims of Christ. The Fortune 500 marketers were entirely correct: by the time young people reach age fourteen, they have made their choices, they are set in their ways, and their worldview is established.

If we want to extend the kingdom of God to the next generation, we have to get it into their heads, and hearts, long before the age of eighteen, even before the age of fourteen. As Luis Bush of the 4/14 Window Global Initiative and others suggest, the critical time is the "4/14 Window," when children are old enough to understand their choice and choose Jesus but not too old to have already had their worldview permanently established. Of course, nothing is permanently set against the gospel, and the Holy Spirit can move a heart of any age to turn to Him. But in generalities we can see that the most efficacious way we can present the next generation to Christ and present Christ to them is to reach them with His Word when they're between the ages of four and fourteen.

ANYA

I've seen how this works in real life time and again. I think of a little girl named Anya in Izhevsk, Russia. When she was six years old, she received our children's Scripture book, the *Book of Hope*, from some Christian children. The book is taken directly from the Scriptures that tells the life story of Jesus and leads children to choose to follow Him. Anya read through her book, and the next time she saw those children, she asked them many questions about Jesus. They invited her to their church, and there she chose to follow Christ as her Savior. Her brother Anton, who was eight, had also received the *Book of Hope*. Anya told him about the church and about her decision. Anton and his friends decided to come to church too, and soon Anton chose to follow Christ.

At home their grandma Rimma was quite curious about the church. She had always been faithful to the Orthodox Church (even during the difficult Soviet days), and she was worried that her grandchildren were part of a cult.

"I must go and see what kind of services you and Anton attend," Rimma said to Anya. "What kind of sect is it?"

"Granny, you must come and see!" Anya said with a smile.

"They don't pray to icons, and there are no candles. What kind of church is that?" Rimma asked. "How can you pray to God without memorizing prayers?"

"Granny, God is everywhere!" Anya said. "You can pray to Him even here. He is alive. My book says this."

"Let me see your book," Rimma said, and began to look at Anya's *Book of Hope*. "Granny, come to church, and maybe you will receive this book," Anya encouraged her.

The next Sunday Rimma did go to church with her grandchildren. She met the pastor and asked him, "Do you believe in God?"

"Yes!" he said. "Do you?"

"Do you believe in Jesus Christ, that He is God and He is risen?" she asked.

"Yes, we do!" the pastor assured her.

"Do you believe in the Holy Trinity?"

"Yes, we do. And you?"

Rimma was surprised to hear these answers. The theology was correct, but here she had found a place where God's love was joyfully celebrated and where every believer could have access to the Father without a memorized prayer or an icon to pray to. She was thrilled.

Rimma's husband, Anya's grandfather, had never believed in God. For years Rimma had prayed that he might come to the Orthodox Church. She had served the priests whenever they needed help at the church. She had burned many candles and prayed reverently memorized prayers for the soul of her husband, but still he refused to go to church or show any interest in spiritual things.

Yet now that Rimma and her grandchildren were attending their new church, they were all praying together for Grandpa. Three months later, impressed by the transformation he had seen in his wife and his grandchildren, Rimma's husband came to church and soon chose to follow Jesus as well! Soon Anya's mother, Natasha, had also come to know Christ.

Rimma and Anya were delighted. Their whole family had chosen to follow Jesus except Anya's uncle, Vladimir. At just twenty-eight years old, he had been sentenced to seven years in prison. They could not see him or bring him to church, but Anya thought they could send him the *Book of Hope* that had first introduced her to Jesus Christ. It was only a children's book, but at that time in Russia, there was very little Christian literature. It was worth a try. Rimma sent the book to her son in prison. Soon she received a letter from Vladimir.

"Mother, thank you for the book. It changed my life. It was as if

I were learning from the ABC book. It opened my eyes! I want to start my life over!"

Soon Vladimir was taking correspondence courses from a Bible school!

Anya's story makes it so clear that very young children can understand the gospel of grace and share their faith. Again and again I have seen how little ones become missionaries to their entire families. It's not that families hear about a great children's ministry and bring the children to church, but rather that the children receive the love of Jesus Christ and pour it out on their families.

Jesus Loves and Values Children

How important are children? They're immeasurably important to Jesus Christ, the Savior who gave His life for them. But the enemy considers them important too. I was recently in Colombia meeting with church leaders who explained that child abandonment was not the main pressing issue in their country. It is child recruitment. The forces of darkness understand their rule and reign is intentioned on capturing the young and using and exploiting them in multiple ways.

War

Did you know, for instance, that according to World Vision, over the course of the war, it's suspected the armed rebels outrageously known as the Lord's Resistance Army in northern Uganda and Congo have kidnapped an estimated thirty thousand to sixty-six thousand children and forced them to serve as frontline soldiers as well as sex slaves and servants?[2] In Africa's many wars through the decades child soldiers have been cannon fodder for government forces and rebel groups alike. The same is true in parts of Asia and Latin America. Some sources say that around the world there are at least three hundred thousand boys and girls forced to fight or die as child soldiers.[3]

Sex

The horrors of prostitution of both boys and girls have been well documented by other ministries who work to rescue them. India, Thailand, and Cambodia—these nations are known as practitioners and suppliers of child sex slaves, but they aren't the only nations where children are forced into hellish lives of relentless sexual abuse. Russia, the former Soviet states, and Eastern Europe are deeply involved in human trafficking. Japan was one of the few developed countries ever placed on the US government's Watch List in the annual report on trafficking in persons back in 2004. It has since been removed from the Watch List but remains a Tier 2 country, which is one not in complete compliance with global regulations to combat human trafficking.[4,5]

Violence

In Asia, Latin America, and the former Soviet Union, gangs that thrive on crime and the drug industry recruit children at younger and younger ages. They infiltrate neighborhoods where children feel forgotten or disenfranchised. Domestic violence and child abuse also takes its toll.

Poverty and disease

The statistics on child hunger, death from preventable disease, and so forth are horrendous—and this is in addition to the ravages of disease. AIDS alone has proven to be an epidemic killer of families and destroyer of children, particularly in sub-Saharan Africa where it has left more than fourteen million children orphaned.[6] These poverty-stricken AIDS orphans have overloaded their nations' systems of government aid and are too numerous to be provided for by surviving extended family. They're often left to raise themselves as best they can and often, used and abused, succumb to HIV themselves as well: globally 91 percent of new HIV infections among children are concentrated in sub-Saharan Africa.[7]

It's clear our enemy, the enemy of their souls, recognizes the importance of children and how critical it is to his diabolical agenda to ensnare them in evil and destruction as early as he can. It should be equally as clear to us, as the church of Jesus Christ, that one of our major, most critical mission fields in this millennium is among the children. Boys and girls in the 4/14 age window desperately need to know the healing, hope, and salvation only Jesus Christ can bring.

Another reason the segment of the world's population in the 4/14 window is so critical to missions, and essentially to the future, is this: children are open, receptive, malleable, and perhaps most importantly, creative. Most little children love to draw, paint, color, play with Play-Doh. They *create*. Most of us growing up are made to feel we're not very good artists, so we quit the "creative stuff." But I truly believe it's to our benefit to help children *retain* their mystery and their urge to create rather than reduce them to something else, something less. American creativity is waning, according to a 2010 *Newsweek* article called "The Creativity Crisis."[8] It's at our own peril that we ignore one of the best sources of creativity in the church and the world today—the children.

The fact that we, as the church, have failed to recognize the inherent value of children—to affect their eternal destinies—and invest in evangelism merely for the sake of bringing the little ones to Jesus is not a new problem. As we read in Scripture, Christ's own disciples made the same mistake. They thought Jesus was too busy to bless the children. But we see His love for the children in Mark 10:13–16:

> People were bringing little children to Jesus to have him touch them, but the disciples rebuked them. When Jesus saw this, he was indignant. He said to them, "Let the little children come to me, and do not hinder them, for the kingdom of God belongs to such as these. I tell you the truth, anyone who will not receive the kingdom of

God like a little child will never enter it." And he took
the children in his arms, put his hands on them and
blessed them.

Our heavenly Father knows the power of a child's life. He loves
the little ones for themselves, and He allows them to become creative agents of change for their families and communities when
they share His love. When we reach children in the 4/14 window
with the life-transforming Word of God, they can reach their families and truly fulfill the Great Commission. Jesus makes it clear.
We hear His words on children and the kingdom again in Matthew
18:2–6:

> I tell you the truth, unless you change and become like
> little children, you will never enter the kingdom of heaven.
> Therefore, whoever humbles himself like this child is the
> greatest in the kingdom of heaven. And whoever welcomes
> a little child like this in my name welcomes me. But if
> anyone causes one of these little ones who believe in me
> to sin, it would be better for him to have a large millstone
> hung around his neck and to be drowned in the depths of
> the sea.

Jesus loves and values children. He came to save them, and
all mankind. Has the church been as desirous of including the
little ones in our efforts? Sadly the answer seems to be no. We've
neglected children for many reasons: they have no power, they
don't pay tithes, their goodwill has little cachet in the market-
place… Even when churches have promoted tremendous children's
ministry, how is the funding of it "sold" to the congregation? By
telling them if there's a good children's ministry, then families will
come in and keep the church growing. The children are seen as the
bridge to their families and the families as the bridge to church
growth.

While we in the church may have neglected missions to children in the past, it's clear we can no longer do so today. Although it is an exaggerated statement to say that Christianity is always only one generation from extinction, it is true that over two or three generations a culture can lose its faith. Look at "post-Christian" Europe, and you'll see the generation that failed to instill in its children a biblical worldview. In his handbook for the 4/14 Window Global Initiative Luis Bush tells us, "I had known that at one time, Europe was the center of Christianity, but in my research, I learned that in 1900, when almost 90 percent of all known followers of Christ lived in Europe, 86 percent of European children attended Sunday school. However, one hundred years later, in the year 2000, only 4 percent of European children did so."[9]

CHILDREN ARE POWERFUL AND EFFECTIVE CHANGE AGENTS

Failure to plant the Word in the minds of the next generation means a failure to pass along the message of salvation and the kingdom values that underpin civilization, as witnessed in much of Europe's death-embracing postmodernism. The moral malaise into which Europe has fallen is evidence of neglecting the admonition to train up a child in the way he should go. But the good news is, it's never too late. The Holy Spirit is always ready, willing, and able to lead us into salvific ministry that can capture the hearts and minds of the *next generation*.

Children are not only a mission field waiting to receive the good news of the gospel; they are also our best hope of global missions for the future. Jesus said, "I praise you, Father, Lord of heaven and earth, because you have hidden these things from the wise and learned, and revealed them to little children. Yes, Father, for this was your good pleasure" (Matt. 11:25–26). It is our Father's *good pleasure* to reveal to little children the truth of His kingdom! He has opened His most intimate wisdom to be shared with the little ones. It's His preference and His good pleasure for them to lead the elders to salvation, new hope, and new life. A little child shall lead them.

The power and effectiveness of children as agents of change is something that's recognized not just by all of us here at OneHope or by the best marketers in international business, but also by our enemy the devil too. The devil wants to attack and destroy children before they have the chance to receive and share the good news.

I believe this was evidenced in a real and terrifying vision God gave to my father back in the 1980s. My dad was then at the helm of a gospel publishing ministry. After a time of intensive prayer and seeking God about the direction the ministry should go, my father had a vision of the world's children suffering a vicious attack of the devil. They were attacked physically with diseases and abuse. They were attacked through poverty and starvation. They were attacked by the violence of war. The terrible scenario broke my father's heart, left him weeping for the next generation that was being so horrifically assaulted. And he heard the Lord tell him, "You must reach the world's children, and you'll do it through leaders." This was really the beginning of the ministry of OneHope, whose vision is "God's Word. Every Child."

The demographics show that globally more than one-third of the population is made up of children and youth. The largest population of children is in poor and developing nations rather than in the developed world. (In fact, in most of the West population is in stagnation or declining. Even in the United States our population growth is coming from the Hispanic population. The CIA World Factbook reports that Latinos make up about 15 percent of our population,[10] and as of 2010, ChildStats.gov reported that among America's children ages zero to seventeen years, 23.1 percent are Latino.[11]) Our missions efforts must focus on children both here at home and around the world.

In India alone there are 248 million children between the ages of five and fourteen. Nigeria, which has half the population of the United States, has more children than we do. Pakistan and

Bangladesh are in the top-ten list of nations with regard to number of children. So you can see, the highest population of our 4/14 mission field are in the most marginalized nations.[12] What we know about believers and nonbelievers alike is that people in general want to see these nations raised out of poverty and want to see social justice achieved for the developing world.

There are no better agents of change to bring social justice to an impoverished nation than the children who will one day lead that nation. Bringing a biblical worldview and a love for Jesus Christ to the next generation in impoverished nations can help to bring that nation out of poverty. The teachings of Jesus Christ, the promise of heaven, and threat of hell are motivations that move families and communities out of poverty. I have witnessed this myself. I'll share those stories later in this book, and I believe you'll be amazed at what God has done and wants to do through the prayers and actions of people like *you*. I hope you're getting ready to join the spiritual revolution!

The Fortune 500 companies I spoke of at the beginning of this chapter wanted to conquer the minds of children by age eight in order to guarantee consumers for life to buy their products. You and I want something so much better for them: the opportunity for them to fulfill their full potential as God's children and come rejoicing into eternity, bringing with them their families, communities, and nations. Surely this demonstrates the importance of children to God and to the church. The 4/14 window is a mission field that cannot be ignored. So let's not ignore it.

Chapter 3

GOD'S WORD IN A WAR ZONE

W<small>E CAN'T IGNORE</small> the fact that the next generation needs Jesus.

I say that my job—or my ministry or my calling—is to fight for the next generation to have the right to receive the most miraculous transformative power in the universe so that their broken hearts and bodies may be healed and their eternal future made secure. And I believe it's an actual fight—spiritual warfare—and a physical battle too. This is also part of my family heritage, the heritage of the miraculous that has shaped my life.

Because I grew up in a war zone.

My parents went to Lebanon in 1965 to launch the Middle East's first Christian television program. I was a baby, my brother was just two, and our sister was born in Lebanon in 1970. As my parents tell the story, miracle after miracle paved the way for my dad and mom to come to Lebanon, pay the broadcast fees, and prepare for a weekly program that would reach throughout the Middle East. Then without warning, just hours before the first program was to be televised, there was an upheaval in the government. The contract and permission to broadcast were rescinded!

For six months my dad beat his head against the brick wall of an uncompromising government, trying to revive the permission and the program all to no avail. Now what? My folks had come to Lebanon under the banner of Middle East Outreach. They'd told their church family back home about the amazing opportunity of Christian TV, and now it was all in shambles. They still wanted to share the Word of God with the region, but most areas just didn't allow preaching and evangelism.

Although the Middle East is the cradle of Christianity, and the disciples of Jesus faithfully spread His Word throughout the region, the church had eventually become rich and ineffectual, losing its passion and fervor. When the followers of the new religion of Islam swept in under the direction of their esteemed prophet, Muhammad, churches fell. If you visit the area now, you'll see many mosques your tour guides will be quick to point out were once Christian churches. Muslims conquered everything from Spain to China, and the Middle East was virtually untouched with the gospel for thirteen hundred years. At one time in Turkey, with a population of more than forty million people, there were only fifty known Christians. One way the Muslims kept anyone from leaving Islam was simply to outlaw any presentation of any other faith and to make it completely illegal to convert.

This was my mom and dad's mission field: a billion Muslims who had never heard the gospel of Jesus. Television had seemed the perfect way to reach the masses. But that dream was dead. Still, God was crafting an important lesson for our family: people respond to His Word, no matter the form, no matter the place. When you touch a life with the Word of God, the Holy Spirit can do His work and begin a transformation.

My parents and their Middle East Outreach team developed a set of six lessons about Christianity that emphasized who Jesus is and His role as Redeemer. They placed advertisements in local Arabic newspapers with intriguing headlines that keyed to current news events that fascinated even Middle Easterners, such as, "He was the most powerful man in the world, but he couldn't stop one assassin's bullet. Will JFK live again? For questions about life, contact PO Box 5724, Beirut, Lebanon" or "She was the most beautiful sought-after woman in the world, but she took her own life. Why did Marilyn Monroe do it? For questions about life, contact PO Box 5724, Beirut, Lebanon."

The ads offered to sign people up for a free correspondence course. The response to this simple campaign was incredible! In less than ten years more than four hundred thousand students from twenty-six Arabic-speaking countries enrolled in the course. By God's grace lives were being transformed on a phenomenal and perhaps even unprecedented scale. Over an eight-year period the Way to Life correspondence school was receiving an average of five hundred letters a month from Arabic people saying they had chosen to follow Christ as Savior. While the ministry was flourishing, conditions in Lebanon were deteriorating. Beirut had been a cosmopolitan city and commercial capital of the region, but civil war, invasions by Syria and Israel, and hostile conflict between Christians and Muslims made it a simmering cauldron from which riots and insurrection might bubble over at any moment. I was witness to attacks by Israel on the refugee camp near where we lived. I knew children who lost their parents in the bombing raids and boys who, then in turn, took up arms to have their revenge on those they saw as oppressors.

Once I was standing on the balcony of our apartment. A Palestinian boy my age—thirteen or fourteen—probably one of those very boys I had played with once upon a time, was carrying a Kalashnikov rifle and staring sullenly out of angry eyes that had already seen too much tragedy in his young life—far more than anyone should see in a lifetime. He pointed the rifle at me, and before I even understood his intention, my father grabbed me and pulled me back inside the house. Would he have killed me? Maybe. War turns children into brutal soldiers. Hate hardens hearts beyond imagination.

I can remember being evacuated by the US Embassy three times during our stay in Lebanon. Our family remained in the United States for several months after the 1971 evacuation until it was deemed safe for us to return to the mission field. My mom, a talented musician, played the organ at the church we attended then. Dick Mills, an evangelist with an amazing prophetic ministry at the time, was preaching there one day. Suddenly he stopped in the middle of his sermon. "The Lord is giving me a word," he said, "for the lady in the blue dress who is playing the organ. Would you stand up?" My mom stood, and the minister reeled off several scriptures that he said the Lord wanted her to remember. They were all promises of protection: "A thousand shall fall at thy side, and ten thousand at thy right hand; but it shall not come nigh thee" (Ps. 91:7, kjv). "For God hath not given us the spirit of fear; but of power, and of love, and of a sound mind" (2 Tim. 1:7, kjv). And so forth. No mention of why she should pay attention, just those words.

Back in Lebanon, with bombs howling all around us more than *two years later,* my mom remembered that word from the Lord.

It was one of the worst civil conflicts ever in Lebanon, literally brother against brother in many cases. The Lebanese army was fighting Palestinian insurgents. Overhead, anti-aircraft artilleries were firing, bullets whizzed by our dining room windows, and mortars exploded in the backyard. That was when my mother grabbed my brother, sister, and me and shepherded us into the bomb shelter in the basement of the apartment building. The other Lebanese women already there with their children were crying and screaming in abject terror.

I don't remember that pandemonium, mind you, but I've heard my mother speak about it. Why is such horror absent from my mind? I was certainly old enough to remember it, and I *do* remember our time in that bomb shelter. I just don't remember being afraid. I know from my mom's stories that she immediately began to pray for peace in the midst of that chaos. And in that moment all the scriptures that Dick Mills had prayed over her came flooding back to her. She began to pray them aloud, and God's peace *did* come into that room.

"Thank God for the obedience of that man to the leading of the

Holy Spirit and for the faithfulness of the Holy Spirit to recall those scriptures to me at the time when I most needed them," my mom says. "I was able to minister to those women in a way I'd never been able to reach them before. I had been a Christian forever, but it amazed me how God preordained me to be there at that time and used Dick Mills to speak into my life an overwhelming sense of what a personal, loving God we have."

As my mom ministered to the Lebanese women in those frightening moments, she also held and comforted my brother and sister and me, reminding us of God's love and power. Looking back, I know my siblings and I never were afraid, even in the scariest situations, because of this fervent faith and this prophetic word that had been spoken over us. Our parents gave us the assurance that we were where God wanted us to be and that this was the safest and best place for us.

I wish you could know my parents—the wonderful, warm, godly people they are. My dad has ministered in more than two hundred nations, and my mom has faithfully gone beside him all over the world. Their first home was a grass hut in Africa with a mud floor. They were roving missionaries together for many years. And because they are such likable people, they were always receiving wonderful gifts from their friends around the world. From Africa they brought home exquisite ivory, back when that was legal. They had beautiful artwork from South America. Our home in Lebanon was a treasure trove of mementos from their worldwide travels together, and a lot of it was very valuable in monetary terms. The apartment in Beirut was really the first place my parents had settled down and lived in one place long enough to display their beautiful things and have a real "home" together and with us children.

ALI

One of my most vivid memories from our time in Lebanon is one dreadful night when we were evacuated. We were always given a plan for evacuation. We were to bring one suitcase—one suitcase for our whole family—and a sack lunch. When the call went out, we were to make our way swiftly and silently to the evacuation point, up a hill where the helicopters could come for us. When this happened, it was important to move fast and try to remain unseen, because our lives were in danger and any delay could be deadly. The last time it happened, the sights and sounds were horrific.

The Israelis had bombed an oil tanker that was burning in a huge conflagration that lit up the night behind us. The smell was terrible—not only the oil fire but also because of the many casualties of war who weren't buried. Because of the curfew there was no time to bury them. They were just piled together and the bodies burned. It was a horrible night. As a firefight lit up other parts of the city, we could see brief glimpses of other expatriate families, sticking to the shadows as best they could as they hurried up the hill to our evacuation point. We were among the very last Americans still in Lebanon.

In the flash of the fire's raging, for a moment the light shone on my dad's face, and I saw that he was laughing. He was laughing out loud. "What's so funny, Bob?" my mom asked him. Remember, we had one suitcase of possessions, our home was likely to be leveled by a bomb blast, and we were running for our lives in the middle of the night.

"Hazel," he said, "do you realize we just left everything we own back in that apartment?"

"Yes, I realize that. Why are you laughing?"

"I was thinking about all those things, and something inside of me just said, *So what?* And I felt so good about that 'So what?' that I just had to laugh."

All those beautiful things, all those valuable things, all those mementos collected over a lifetime of ministry—they were just *stuff.* The really important things we would never leave behind. The eternal, the unseen—those were the important things. Growing up in a war zone, this is what I learned: "So we fix our eyes not on what is seen, but on what is unseen. For what is seen is temporary, but what is unseen is eternal" (2 Cor. 4:18). The home and the possessions we left behind were never as real as the eternal souls we had impacted with the love of Jesus Christ.

All around us that night people were moving in our same direction, when suddenly, out of the darkness, an Arab family came running toward us. There was no reason for them to be out of the bomb shelter on this night. They came looking for us just to say good-bye. They were risking their lives to say thank you to my mom and dad. With them was a seventeen-year-old boy named Ali. He too wanted to say thank you. Although, when you think about it, it might be hard to see why he was grateful. Because of my parents' work he had been rejected by his family and thrown out of his house. His grandfather wanted to kill him and had put a death contract (a *fatwa*) on him. He was living in the basement of this other Christian family so his own relatives couldn't find and kill him.

But that was his message: "Thank you." "*Shukran, shukran.*" He had chosen to follow Jesus through my dad's ministry. To his Muslim family this was anathema. But for him it was the greatest joy he had ever known. Not only was he risking his life to be seen on the streets where relatives might find and attack him, he was also risking his life in a bombing raid to come out and try to find my parents, to hug my dad and say to my mom, "Thank you for coming here to tell us about Jesus!"

At that time I was obviously too young to truly understand the joy in my father's heart as we left our home and all that we owned, but I understand it now. We had been privileged to affect Ali's destiny forever. What greater gift could we have given him? It was worth all our stuff, worth this stealthy run for cover in the middle of the night, to know we'd been part of his transformation.

Fawzi

I didn't know it at the time, but a boy a few years older than me was cowering in his own apartment in Beirut that night, unable to evacuate because there was nowhere for *him* to go. He was a local. This was his war. No helicopters would whisk him away to safety. So Fawzi spent weeks inside his apartment, with only brief periods of cease-fire, when it was possible to go out into the streets and shop for food—and look for something to read. Fawzi was preparing for university, and these weeks with no access to books, magazines, or newspapers were brutal for him. During one cease-fire he actually began digging through the heaps of garbage in the street, hoping someone had thrown out something he would like to read. What he found was a bundle of *Way to Life* magazines, which were published as part of my dad's correspondence school ministry. He greedily took them back to his apartment. Finally he had something new to read as he waited out the fighting!

He read them all, many times. As a Muslim he had heard of Jesus only as a prophet, and not even a very important one. But Muslims have a great respect for the printed page, and what Fawzi read in the magazines spoke directly to his heart. He began to believe that Jesus was more than a prophet, that He was the Son of God and God Himself! He chose to follow Christ as Savior, right there, alone, in his apartment, in a war zone.

I only know Fawzi's story because, a few years later, my dad was speaking at a church in Rockford, Illinois, where he met Fawzi. Whoever had thrown away the magazines he had found had also, for some reason, cut out all the reply forms and addresses of the Way to Life correspondence school or Middle East Outreach Center, which was my dad's church in Lebanon. Fawzi hadn't known how to get in touch with any other Christians—until his parents sent him to the United States to university. (The schools in Lebanon had closed during the war.) His first mission when he arrived in Rockford was to find a church where other people believed in Jesus and worshipped Christ as he did. Then he began inviting other expatriates from the Middle East to come to church with him, and many of them came to know Christ as Savior too.

When he heard that the man who had founded Way to Life was coming to his church, he was excited to share his story! The magazines in someone else's trash had brought him to new life in Christ. God's Word in a war zone transforms lives. God's Word *anywhere* transforms lives. By the way, Fawzi brought a group of other students with him to that meeting—students whom he had led to the Lord and whom he was discipling. That's the power of God's Word to transform.

Natasha

I've seen it many times in my own life and ministry. For a time as I was starting out with the OneHope organization, I was traveling in and out of Russia often, collaborating with our church partners, helping forge new relationships, opening new frontiers for ministry. It brings to my mind a young woman named Natasha and her story of transformation, which flowed from an encounter with the Word of God. She was one of those little girls in Russia whose father was enslaved to alcohol. She didn't care. She loved him.

But when he died from complications of his addiction, she was heartbroken. She took no comfort from the rest of the family. In fact, she despised her four brothers, and she felt that they hated her. As the only girl in the family and her papa's favorite, she'd always received the best of everything. Her brothers were jealous. But she, in turn, was jealous of her younger brother, the baby of the family, who was born when she was already twelve years old. She hated the way the new baby took her parents' attention from her!

Natasha had already begun following in her father's footsteps before he died. She had begun drinking and smoking when she was only thirteen. Since she'd been displaced as the baby of her family, she didn't want anyone thinking of her as a baby anymore. She wanted to show everyone that she was old enough to do whatever she wanted.

But that wasn't unusual in her small village outside Gainy, Russia. The rural area had once been the site of collective farms during the Soviet era, and most people worked on the farms. But when the USSR dissolved, the collectives shut down. Work became scarce—in fact, it was losing his job that set Natasha's father on the path to drinking himself to death. Unable to provide for his family and despairing about the future, he had completely surrendered to alcohol. Her mom struggled to provide for the family, and Natasha went her own way.

"I can say I acted as a hooligan," she recalls.

The future at that moment looked bleak indeed for Natasha. Statistics show that many young Russian women in her position end up pregnant, perhaps having an abortion, even multiple abortions, or becoming addicted to drugs or alcohol. But something happened that changed the trajectory of Natasha's young life. She saw a poster at the convention center in her town advertising a three-day youth festival. The funny part was that the "youth" festival was going to be sponsored by some Christian organization, and the only Christians Natasha had ever seen or heard of were old grandmas in long dresses and head scarves who lit candles and kissed icons in the dark recesses of the Orthodox Church. How on earth could those old ladies put on a *youth festival*?

She was so perplexed by the very notion that she didn't even bother going to the first day of the festival, but a friend came and got her the next day, telling her that the event was fun and interesting and that there were lots of friendly young people. Reluctantly Natasha went, and she was amazed by what she discovered. The teenagers and young adults who welcomed her were cheerful, outgoing, and seemed very happy. And they weren't even drinking! This was so unusual in Gainy. No one was ever this happy.

The upbeat music they presented that night was wonderful, and the speakers who told about their lives with Christ sounded so genuine, so joyful. Natasha knew that she wanted for herself whatever secret they had. They gave her the *Book of Hope* to tell her more about Jesus, and she prayed to become a follower of Christ that very night.

"I read the *Book of Hope* completely through, and I liked the fact that I found many answers to my multiple questions. We had a New Testament at home, and I had looked at it once before, but it was very hard to read. The book I received that evening had pictures, interesting articles, and most importantly, it was easy to read; that is why I read it to the end."

Natasha and several of her friends began attending the church that had partnered with OneHope to sponsor the youth festival. She found she was warmly welcomed there, just as she had been at the festival, and soon she was singing in the choir and looking for ways to minister to others. She and her friends eventually joined the team that went to other villages to put on festivals and give away the *Book of Hope*.

Later she attended Bible school and has served on various ministry teams at her church, always telling other young people all that Christ has done for her. Her little brother, the "baby" of whom she was once jealous, has now chosen to follow Jesus too and attends church with Natasha. Miraculously, her relationships with all her brothers, and with her mother, have been healed too, and now they treasure their family ties. The young girl, this "hooligan" as she called herself, who started drinking at age thirteen and once seemed on the path to destruction, is now on the path to abundant and eternal life because the biblical message of purpose and hope was presented to her, and it showed her a better way.

What a privilege for me to have played some small part in providing the good news that affected her destiny forever! But I wasn't the one who gave her the book, and I probably wasn't the one who paid for that book. I told you before that I believe God intends each of His children to be people of destiny and to affect the destiny of others. Someone in the United States made the commitment to give the funds that provided *Kniga Zhezn* (the Russian-language *Book of Hope*), someone in Russia made the commitment to take the book to the village of Gainy, and someone somewhere was praying for Russia's next generation. All together we affected destiny for Natasha, forever.

My history, heritage, and experience as a minister have all shown me miraculous stories of lives transformed. Now I am showing them to you, because it's *your* heritage to be part of this ongoing miracle too. It's *your* heritage as a child of God.

My own life too has been transformed, in its turn, by the power and love of Jesus Christ. The next three chapters will unpack that journey, starting with the sweetest part of it—the story of Kim, my amazing wife, and me.

Chapter 4

ROB AND KIM

You've seen the heritage of the miraculous that shaped my life. So I know you will believe that God uniquely prepared the woman for me—a wife who shares my missionary DNA in every way. Kim Bueno grew up on the mission field as part of an evangelistic clan that has helped to bring thousands of people to faith in Christ and disciple them in that faith. Her family, like mine, had a tradition of transformation. Her grandparents went to Cuba as missionaries in the 1920s. Her parents, Elmer and Lee Bueno, were pioneer missionaries in Latin America. Her uncle and aunt, John and Lois Bueno, are also renowned missionaries of the Assemblies of God fellowship. John planted one of the largest churches in the world in El Salvador; pioneered Latin America ChildCare, which feeds, clothes, and educates tens of thousands of children annually; and became director of World Missions for the Assemblies of God. Kim and her brother, Chris, were raised on the mission field, constantly following God's call on their parents' lives.

We were destined for each other, especially because our parents were good friends and her folks made her "pray through" whenever she had doubts or misgivings during our courtship.

My father was the minister who led one of the first Youth With A Mission teams in history to the Bahamas in 1964. Now known as YWAM, this great missions organization deploys young believers all over the world to share the good news. Then just a few weeks later Kim's dad, Elmer Bueno, led another YWAM trip to the Dominican Republic. Her dad and my dad were best friends and had stood up in each other's weddings.

Both Kim and I were reared with a missional heritage that we knew we wanted to pursue. Kim, though, has a mother's heart. What she wanted for her own children was a more stable life, a home where they could always find their bearings and foundation. To her credit she knew that if we established a home in the United States once we began our family, there was a good chance we would often be separated. Especially as I grew into my position at OneHope, my travels were to become lengthy and frequent. She agreed to make this sacrifice, for the sake of our calling and the sake of our children. I can truly say that I wouldn't be who I am today or where I am today if it weren't for my beloved wife. I know her reward will be great.

I can also say that the direction of my life and ministry would not be the same today were it not for my friendship with her father. Elmer and Lee Bueno were pioneer media and crusade missionaries in Latin America. They became hosts of the *PTL Club* for Latin America and subsequently launched their own television program, a cutting-edge hit throughout the continent. They had an inflatable tent nearly the size of a football field called Cathedral of Air, which they would set up in various locations and conduct amazing outreaches. They introduced thousands of people to Jesus and helped launch new churches. But an even more powerful part of their ministry was *Buenos Amigos,* their Spanish-language television program. (It means "Good Friends," but of course it was a play on Elmer's name.) This program helped bring Christian TV to Latin America and drew an audience of about twenty-five million people in sixteen Spanish-speaking nations.

Getting to know Elmer and witnessing the power of media ministry sparked an epiphany for me. Growing up in Lebanon among Muslim people who had such great respect for books and witnessing firsthand how correspondence courses had helped to spread the gospel in a region very resistant to any faith but Islam, I was in tune with the power of God's Word *on the printed page.* I'd heard my dad preach again and again about the power of the printed page. How the communist revolution in China had really been won by the circulation of communist literature long before the war began. How the USSR had exported its philosophy throughout Africa and Latin America by publishing Marxist literature to fuel revolutionary fires. How even the so-called "romance novel" in the United States had turned a generation of women on to immorality and soft pornography. I knew the power of the printed page.

However, my father-in-law, Elmer, knew the power of media ministry.

He helped show me that the Word of God is not just a Bible. Jesus is the living Word, and wherever, however, we present Him, He transforms lives. When my dad first founded the ministry of OneHope, all we had was the *Book of Hope,* a printed book or magazine with scriptures that told the life of Christ and included some added sections to help children and youth come to faith in Him. Of course it worked (and still works today). It was the Word of God! But for children who can't read or don't read or for places where books are scarce, Elmer Bueno showed me another way to present the Word.

We needed *more* than the printed page.

In the years since this epiphany, OneHope has grown to embrace many different presentations of the gospel of Jesus Christ, the living Word, and to this day the results continue to astound me. Among the many thousands touched and transformed: Sonika, a little girl in India.

SONIKA

Sonika wanted to know about Jesus.

Her mistake was asking her mom for answers.

They're Hindus, and what little knowledge her mother had about

Jesus and Christianity sounded very muddled to Sonika. Of course, in their traditional Hindu faith there are many gods, and Sonika couldn't make out what made Jesus so special and why Christians worshipped Him alone. Her mother's explanation shed no light on the subject, and Sonika came away with the impression that Jesus was not for Indian people at all.

The reason Sonika, a ten-year-old Hindu girl, was looking for Jesus? She had no peace. There was turmoil in her own heart and nothing but fighting and arguments in her home. Her father drank too much then came home and picked fights with her mother. The two of them went at it, and Sonika felt abandoned and alone, falling asleep, when she could sleep, to the sounds of shouting and angry insults hurled between her parents. The Hindu gods didn't help her. Sonika had begun to doubt them. Maybe Jesus could help, but after what her mother told her, she doubted that too.

In fact, she'd begun to think there must not be any God, or she wouldn't be allowed to suffer this way. What hope did she have? How could her future ever be any better?

Things began to change for Sonika on the morning a friend invited her to a church outside their village where a children's program was taking place. There were songs, Bible stories, dramas, and lots of fun, all based around the development of good moral values.

"Everything we learned was so new for me," Sonika remembers. "I was so happy and excited to learn. I was very much blessed to be there."

Then a film showing began: OneHope's life of Christ film, *The GodMan*. The Indian version of the film also has a live-action introduction and conclusion that follows two modern-day Indian children who are determined to run away from home until they meet a stranger who tells them about Jesus and the difference He can make in their lives. The animation was also contextualized to present characters and settings more familiar to Indian audiences; even Jesus looks as if He could be an Indian man. The soundtrack too was redone to appeal to Indian children and youth.

For Sonika it worked! No more could she think of Jesus as someone who wasn't for Indian people. As soon as she saw Him on the screen, she began to understand who He was and what His life meant. It made so much more sense than what her mother had told her!

"I began to realize that Jesus is the only true God, the only powerful and the living God. I knew I had to confess I am a sinner, and I ought to believe only in Jesus for salvation," Sonika says. "If Jesus loves the murderers, I believe Jesus loves me too. So I don't have to be insecure and lonely, because I strongly believe Jesus would walk beside me and would restore peace and happiness in my family."

Sonika chose to follow Jesus Christ and has remained faithful to her commitment. She even shared the gospel story with her family and helped her mother understand the truth about Jesus. Her pastor and the people from her church visit her home and speak with her parents often, and Sonika is praying her mom and dad will soon choose to follow Christ too.

Sonika's story illustrates what I learned from Elmer and Lee Bueno: you don't have to put a Bible in someone's hands to tell them about Jesus. You can impart a biblical message of purpose and hope and clearly show the gospel's message of Christ's love, death, and resurrection in many different ways.

And *The GodMan* film has proven itself a powerful tool for ministry in India in the months and years since Sonika first encountered it. We had the amazing opportunity to broadcast the film one Easter season and the following Christmas, first on cable television and then on India's national TV network. Local pastors and believers rallied together for a broad outreach across the country. They prepared for home showings by inviting their neighbors to come and watch the film with them. Churches also sponsored big-screen showings of the broadcast and invited the whole community. Local believers and churches also used VCDs (like DVDs for the Indian subcontinent) to present the film. And after the film showing, they discussed the life of Christ and gave the children and youth the *Book of Hope*. Children in school received an age-appropriate edition, and younger children or illiterate children received the Storying Edition *Book of Hope*, which uses illustrations from the film.

The scope of these TV outreaches was beyond anything we could have imagined or engineered. Literally millions of lives were touched. The numbers for home showings alone are dramatic: about 5,573,345 children and family members watched the telecast at the home of Christian neighbors or at a church outreach event. Another 1,688,597 saw the film at a VCD showing in a church or a home of Christians. Our partners recorded more than 1.78 million children and youth chose to follow Christ as Savior.

I'm not usually a big fan of anything like "conversion numbers." I remember sitting at lunch with several ministry heads and one fellow who was reputed to be quite a large donor of funding to charitable causes. One after another the other presidents and principals were sharing their excitement over their numbers reached and the plans they had for the future. They were very committed, dedicated people who I know were sincere and only wanted the funds in order to carry out God's call on their lives and ministries. But that kind of talk just isn't my thing. At the time OneHope had just presented the *Book of Hope* to the two hundred fifty millionth child to receive it (as you read this, we're in pursuit of our one *billionth*), but I wasn't saying much.

Finally one of the other guys turned to me and said, "You just hit a big milestone, didn't you, Rob?" I acknowledged what had happened, but I felt obliged to add that we're not really about the numbers at OneHope. We're interested in each individual child and in knowing that in the life of each one, the gospel wasn't just presented but was received, understood, and acted upon.

That's why I feel OK telling you about the India outreach and the 1.78 million children who came to Christ because of it. These decisions were recorded by trained children's workers who had been prepared not only to lead children to Christ but also to disciple them right there in their homes and local churches. In the months since, by God's grace, we've seen wonderful transformations taking place. And I believe this may have been the largest and most effective, single, unified outreach to children at any time in missions history.

Sonika's story is the human face of it, the individual child whom Jesus knows and loves and whose destiny has been forever affected by the power of His Word.

ELIENNE

Another example is Elienne from Haiti. Most people in Haiti say they're Catholic. A lot of them also still practice voodoo. And the dirty little secret of many of the most impoverished families is that they sell their children into slavery. Little girls become domestic help or, tragically, even sex slaves.

That's what happened to Elienne. Her family struggled to put food on the table. If they gave Elienne to an "uncle" in another town, he would pay them handsomely for her, and it would mean one less mouth to feed. Elienne wanted to believe that her parents thought she would just be working for him as a maid, but it's more likely they understood exactly what her fate would be.

This new "uncle" moved Elienne into his home and began sexually abusing her when she was just a small girl. The hellish abuse went on until Elienne was old enough to run away and make her way back to her parents' home. She believed once her parents knew what had happened to her, they would feel sorry they had sent her away and happy that she had managed to return home. But she was wrong. They were angry and told her how bad she had been to run away. After all, a deal was a deal. She belonged to the "uncle" now, and they were no better equipped to provide for her than when she left.

Elienne was devastated.

She felt dirty, unwanted, and unloved.

And she knew that no one would ever love her now.

If her own parents did not want her, no one ever would.

Her parents refused to allow her to stay with them. They couldn't feed her. They thought they'd gotten rid of her. Thankfully another woman in the neighborhood gave Elienne a place to stay, but she was also very poor. Now Elienne, just a young teen and bankrupt of all hope and self-esteem, was desperate to help bring money into the home and to provide for herself so she could attend school. So she did all she knew to do: she began to prostitute herself.

But one day a team from the local church came to her school with a gift for each student, the *Book of Hope*. The believers put on a presentation for the students, which included a little drama designed to show young people like Elienne just how much God loves them. To this day Elienne remembers it clearly.

First, a young man offered a lollipop to one of the students, but just as he was handing it over, he dropped it in the dirt and it became filthy. Did the student still want it? No, of course not; it was disgusting!

Next he substituted a dollar bill for the lollipop, and again, as he went to hand it over, he dropped it into the dirt. He bent and picked up the filthy dollar and inquired whether the student still wanted it as it was now all dirty. But of course a dirty dollar is still a dollar, and of course it was still wanted!

"He explained that even though the lollipop lost its value when it became dirty, young people like me were like the dollar bill to God," Elienne recalls. "No matter how many times we fall and get dirty, we never lose our value in the eyes of God. The young man reminded us God loves us and that we are important to the One who created us."

This was an eye-opening moment for the teenage girl!

She had been feeling as if she were worthless and had no value because of what had happened to her as a child and the way she had been living since she returned to her neighborhood. But here was amazing good news: God didn't care how filthy she felt. He still valued her as a beloved child!

"I began to feel hopeful about my troubled life," she says. "Vionel, one of the young men in the group, made me realize there was a person who wanted to become my friend. He told us Jesus, the Son of God, wanted to become our friend and help us with our problems. At that moment I decided to begin walking with Jesus. Truly, Jesus is the best friend I've ever had! He has taken all my sadness and given me a new eternal joy. Yes, He is a good friend!"

Today at age nineteen Elienne is no longer involved in prostitution. She has the support of a loving church family to help her, and she is committed to Jesus Christ. She attends church, studies the Word, and has even been sharing the gospel with her parents in hopes that they too will one day discover the same joy Jesus has brought to her.

Elienne received God's Word just by watching a little drama and receiving the *Book of Hope* and is being nurtured in her local church. But her story illustrates how we can introduce Jesus through a drama or show Him to someone through TV. That's what the Buenos did through their TV ministry in Latin America, and it's what OneHope does everywhere *The GodMan* film is shown.

The ways that you, personally, can affect destiny for the next generation are everywhere! If you're looking for the best way you can help to transform the future by God's power, I want to encourage you to start by sharing the Word with children and youth.

I've witnessed it in my own life; I've witnessed it in my father's ministry—children and youth are, by far, the most likely to respond to the gospel, and they are definitely those most in need of God's loving touch and protection. Don't let this moment of decision pass you by. Consider this a call to action: help to reach the children. You can affect their destiny forever.

Just as my life with Elmer and Lee Bueno's daughter was the perfect fit for me, engineered by God for my happiness and for the genesis of our two wonderful daughters, my involvement with the ministry of OneHope was also my destiny—although it took me some time to get there. I want to show you how God used struggle and trial, blindness, and yes, even miracles to get me there. I think it's a story that may resonate with you, if you've ever struggled to understand why.

Chapter 5

ONCE I WAS BLIND

EYES ARE THE Achilles' heel of the Hoskins family. My father is blind in one eye, and like him, I've been able to see well out of only one eye for years. But nothing prepared me for the morning I woke up unable to see out of my "good eye."

My oldest daughter, Diandra, was just fifteen days old. Kim and I had accepted an appointment as missionaries to Cote d'Ivoire (Ivory Coast) to share the love of Christ with Muslim university students. Suddenly all was in peril. I couldn't see a thing.

It did not occur to me then, in my panic and confusion, that this physical blindness was a reflection of spiritual blindness on my part. God had given me an amazing glimpse of powerful global ministry just a few months before, and I had failed to see the potential.

Kim and I had been youth ministers in California at the time the ministry of OneHope was just getting off the ground. It was expanding from its original effort to give God's Word to every schoolchild in El Salvador and was beginning to reach out to other Spanish-speaking nations as well. My dad invited me to bring a team of young people from our church to help distribute the *Book of Hope* in Honduras. This kind of ministry was all new to my dad. He had been a child preacher, and naturally other grown-ups and adult ministers had assumed he ought to preach to other children. But this was not what God had called him to do, and he resisted this pressure. In fact, because he was homeschooled and spent his childhood as a traveling evangelist, he never knew much about other children. Children's ministry had never attracted him at all. He was thrust into it by this new vision, and the Holy Spirit led Him every step of the way, opening wonderful doors in country after country.

Honduran schools had opened their doors, allowing teams to come in to conduct assemblies and present the gospel. It was a great opportunity for the students in our youth ministry to experience, so of course we signed on. But this was my dad's thing. This was his vision, his ministry. I didn't have any ownership of OneHope or the idea of what the ministry's vision, "God's Word. Every Child," actually meant. Perhaps the downside of having an illustrious father is that if a son isn't careful to stay close to Christ and listen for his own calling, he may endeavor to prove himself on his own and go his own way. I was proud of my dad. I was excited about the newly formed ministry (at the time, it was called *Book of Hope*), but I didn't see my future there. I'd been raised in Lebanon among Muslim young people, I spoke French very well, and Francophone Africa was where I thought God could best use me.

Then I went to Honduras. The program was to conduct school assemblies, and our team was sent to the largest high school in Latin America in Tegucigalpa, Honduras. All day long we conducted assembly after assembly, distributing thousands of copies of the *Book of Hope* and talking about the difference Jesus had made in our lives. It was great for the students from the United States to have this opportunity, and I know, by God's grace, we touched many young lives during that time. I was happy to be doing this. I had no idea of the impact we were making.

CARLOS

There was a boy who went to that school named Carlos. His father had died, and his mother had struggled for years to provide for

Carlos and his little brothers and sisters. They were hungry all the time. He'd been reading the Marxist literature that flooded Latin America at the time, and he had come to believe the government was responsible for his poverty and hunger. He'd bought the Marxist philosophy because he wanted a better life for his mother and little siblings. On the weekends this boy went into the countryside to a training camp for terrorists. He was planning to help overthrow the government. He was learning how to make bombs, how to shoot guns, and how to prepare for the moment when he and his fellow terrorists would take up arms in a bloody revolution! He received the *Book of Hope* the first day we ministered at his high school.

We came back a second day because the school was so huge. We were going to reach a total of about seventeen thousand students in the area with the good news. I thought this was great. How else could we have impacted so many lives in such a short amount of time? But I didn't really understand the impact we were making, not until Carlos caught me as we were getting off the bus for our second day of ministry.

"Yesterday you handed me this book, and I took it home and read it," Carlos told me. He understood the story of Jesus's birth and life. When he read about the crucifixion, he understood that, because of course his family was nominally Catholic and he was used to seeing Jesus Christ on the cross.

"But then I read that Jesus was raised from the dead," he said to me. "I came here to ask you today, was He really raised from the dead? Is Jesus alive?"

"Carlos, Jesus is alive," I was privileged to tell this seventeen-year-old boy. By this time tears were running down his face. I was able to pray with him right there, and he accepted Christ into his life. I was able to introduce him to a local pastor and church that would come around and support him and his family, discipling them in the faith.

This thing we were doing in Honduras, this presenting of God's

Word to young people, it had the power to transform young lives—
and shape the future of nations! It was changing a teenager from a
terrorist into a follower of Christ! I experienced this firsthand. I
really believe this was God's moment to awaken me to a lifetime
calling of engaging the next generation with a biblical message of
purpose and hope. But somehow I didn't see it then.

I went home. I continued in youth ministry at my church until
I received the call to missions, and Kim and I agreed to accept
the appointment to Cote d'Ivoire. We had our baby girl, and two
weeks later I woke up unable to see out of my good eye. The world
was dark to me.

OBEDIENCE. TRUST. FAITH.

Kim rushed me to the eye doctor, and specialists told me there
was very little they could do. My retinas were too thin. One was
completely detached, and the other was about to detach. They per-
formed an emergency surgery to try to save the one eye. But this
surgery required six weeks of recovery, and during the entire six
weeks I had to lie prone with my face down to keep the retina
still in hopes it would heal. And there was no guarantee of success.
They wouldn't know if it had worked until the six weeks ended, and
I stood up. There was every possibility that once I stood, I would be
blind. I can't even describe to you the anguish in my heart during
this time. What if I could never see my baby daughter again? What
if I couldn't provide for my family?

I cried out to God, "Why did You put this missionary calling on
my life if I won't be able to go?"

The first surgery did not cure me, and over the course of an
entire year, I went through six surgeries. I should have known that
in the Christian walk there is no struggle that does not also offer
a gift of grace. Mine arrived one night when I was at my lowest.
Kim came into the room where I was lying facedown and placed
her hands on me and began to pray. The presence of Jesus filled the

room so strongly, and I felt the Savior covering me completely with Himself, with His love. He began to take me on a journey through three particular scriptures that illuminated my situation.

First, He brought to my mind the passage in Acts where Saul, "the soon-to-be apostle Paul," is on the road to Damascus. He has been stricken by the light of God, knocked to the ground, and he calls out to this Jesus, this God he doesn't know or believe in: "Lord, what do You want me to do?" (Acts 9:6, NKJV). It was so clear to me. Jesus was saying He wanted my obedience. I knew Jesus wanted me to pray the same prayer Saul prayed and ask Him simply, "What do You want me to do?"

The problem, though, was that I wasn't "murderous Saul," setting out on the road to Damascus to kill Christians. I was a missionary from a family of missionaries, who wanted nothing more than to share the message of salvation with people in need! I wasn't a sinner like Saul; I didn't need Jesus to knock me down to get my attention. I wanted to present His gospel to Muslims! Why should He be telling me now that what He wanted was my obedience? Why ask Him what He wanted me to do? I'd already received the call to missions, but I couldn't go because of my blindness! Basically I wanted to tell Jesus how great I was, about all the sacrifices I'd made—but then for Him to treat me this way and let me suffer through this blindness when I was all ready to go and serve Him in Africa.

Then I heard the voice of the Lord saying to me, "Look, I am not interested in your sacrifices. I would like you to come before Me with nothing, with no preconceived notions, no plans of what you're going to 'do for Me,' and just say, *Lord, what do You want me to do?*"

Then I understood.

Yes, God had uniquely prepared me for ministry and given me a wonderful heritage of the miraculous, of missions and evangelism, but my qualifications were nothing to Him. He didn't want me to lean on my background, my family, my connections. He wanted me to lean on Him alone and come before Him with nothing but a willingness to obey.

This easily led into the next lesson He had for me, as He brought to mind Proverbs 3:5 (KJV): "Trust in the Lord with all thine heart; and lean not unto thine own understanding." I felt Him telling me, "You rely on yourself. You are relying on your heritage, on your ability to preach, on your connections, on who your father, father-in-law, and uncles are.... You really don't think you need Me. You don't know what it means to trust in Me."

He was showing me that I'd never really learned to trust Him, because I'd never really had to. All my life my family and faith had shaped me to be a missionary, and there had never been the least struggle about it. I *loved* Jesus, but I'd never had to *trust* Jesus. Two very different things.

God had one more lesson to impart to me on this night. He directed my mind to the story of the blind man Jesus healed in Mark 8:23–25 (NKJV):

> So He took the blind man by the hand and led him out of the town. And when He had spit on his eyes, and put His hands on him, He asked him if he saw anything. And he looked up and said, "I see men like trees, walking." Then He put His hands on his eyes again, and made him look up. And he was restored and saw every man clearly.

This was Jesus's way to tell me about faith—faith that my own healing was coming, but it wouldn't happen all at once. From this moment Kim and I had faith in a transitional healing that would bring my sight back. This was so important because, throughout that year, my sight continued to deteriorate, but we had the promise of Christ that healing was coming. When you look at the story of the blind man, you have to wonder, "Why did it take a second touch from Jesus? Didn't He have the power to heal the blind man?" Of course He did. Based on my experience, I believe

Jesus was simply teaching a lesson through this progressive type of healing. Certainly it taught me a lesson.

I can still relive that night in my mind and feel the love Jesus poured out on me and the promises He gave me and the lessons He taught me—lessons of obedience, trust, and faith. As beautiful as this rich spiritual experience was, I still had many long days of surgery and recovery ahead of me. I couldn't work, and we rapidly ran out of funds. Kim's parents had graciously taken us in, but I knew my family was living on credit. Kim tried to keep the brutal truth from me about our finances, but at one point I just made her tell me: How bad is it? What do we owe? The amount back at that time was shocking, especially because we had a new baby and no money coming in. We were in debt $1,850.

But now I had God's promise that I could—and must—trust in Him completely. Kim and I were praying and claiming the promises of provision, when I got a phone call from Pastor Ron Prinzing. His church had, at that time, supported my dad's ministry for about thirty years. He said he'd felt prompted to lead his church to pray for me that Sunday morning, and he'd told the congregation that I was battling blindness and struggling financially because of it. That was all he said from the pulpit, and he prayed for me. But he said that after the service, people spontaneously began to come up and give him checks made out to me, gifts for Kim and me. He sent all of the checks to us. The grand total—$1,850, the exact amount of our need!

I knew God had not abandoned us. I knew He was our source and my healing was sure.

I still remember a nurse removing the bandages after my sixth surgery. Usually my eyes are so bad that I can't even read the gigantic E at the top of the eye chart—I can't see it. As the bandages came off and I looked at the chart, I could read every letter. The nurse was flabbergasted! She ran to get the doctor. He cautioned me that I was still on medication, that my eyes were dilated, and this excellent vision probably wouldn't last. But I just said, "No, I told you the Lord was going to heal me, and He has."

I still had struggles, but today I have implants in my eyes, and my vision is 20/25. God has power to heal, and He did heal me.

That was a hellish year for Kim and me, but honestly, we would not trade it because of what we learned. Kim and I grew into our own grasp of obedience, trust, and faith. Never again would we rely on the missionary heritage we shared or the contacts we had in our fellowship. We learned, as never before, to rely on God alone. Those three lessons I learned—obedience, trust, and faith—have guided my every step from that moment forward. Every morning I ask the Lord, "What would You have me do? I trust You, and whatever You say, I am going to do. And by faith I believe it will happen." The last thing I do before I go to bed at night is say, "Lord, I did my best to do what You wanted today." Or if I haven't, I acknowledge that, and I know that He'll give me a new chance the next day.

Perhaps inevitably people heard about this miraculous healing and how God had brought me through such difficult trials. Doors opened for me to share the story and preach at various churches and venues across the United States and even overseas. Many times I was able to go some place as a traveling evangelist and collaborate with our contacts in that country to help Dad's *Book of Hope* project get going. Slowly the Lord revealed to me *this* was the direction He had planned for me all along. This wasn't just Dad's vision. Because the directive to engage every child and youth with the gospel was going to outlive Dad, this was *my vision* too. I just hadn't been able to see it.

Carlos's dramatic transformation had also been right in front of me. I had witnessed the life-transforming power of God's Word, but back then I had not learned to trust Jesus completely. I had continued to go my own way, the way I thought I should go with my skill set and my background. I was blind to my real calling.

This is why I bless that year of struggle and pain. Ultimately, it brought me to my destiny.

What Is Your Destiny?

What about you? Have you discovered your calling and your destiny? What I have learned in my years with OneHope is that every believer can be one who affects destiny. I happened to be the one in Honduras who handed Carlos the *Book of Hope*, but someone else had paid for the book to be sent there for him, someone else had organized the local believers and our teams for ministry in school that day, and someone else had prayed that our team would impact Honduran boys and girls. Every single believer can affect destiny, one way or another, and become a person of purpose in building God's kingdom. Are you affecting destiny for anyone today? Are you teaching your children or grandchildren why it's important to share their faith? You can and you should and you must. It's not that difficult. I don't want you to have to go through another day of spiritual blindness when I've already walked that road, and I can tell you from experience God wants you to be part of affecting destiny for those who haven't yet been able to receive the good news.

The vision of "God's Word. Every Child" has become powerfully imprinted on my heart and mind. Out of that darkness and blindness I finally realized the ministry God had birthed in the heart of my father was to become the focal point of *my* life and ministry as well. It was my destiny. What's yours?

Chapter 6

NOW I SEE

I N SO MANY ways going blind was a metaphor for the direction in which the Lord was to lead me. When you can't see, you begin to sense things that are unseen; that's the best way I can describe it. And that very moment when Jesus dealt with me about trusting in Him was when I began to realize the importance of the unseen, even in our "seen" world.

As I came out of that year of trials, 2 Corinthians 4:17–18 became my life verse: "For our light and momentary troubles are achieving for us an eternal glory that far outweighs them all. So we fix our eyes not on what is seen, but on what is unseen. For what is seen is temporary, but what is unseen is eternal."

While I was blind, something *unseen* had broken into our visible world and reshaped my ideas about what it means to serve God. From the moment I officially became part of the OneHope team, I knew I had found my lifetime calling. My father had launched this ministry in 1987 after an intensive six-week period in which God had burdened his heart for children. As I told you before, he had never wanted to do children's ministry. Even as a child he'd never understood other young people very well. How unusual for him that at the age of fifty-one he should suddenly receive this word from the Lord: "I want My Word taken to the children and youth of the world."

Some months later the minister of education for the nation of

El Salvador contacted my dad, who was then the president of the largest Christian foreign language publishing house, to ask for the Scriptures for every schoolchild in El Salvador: 968,000 children and youth. And my dad said yes! He saw this as the open door to begin reaching the children and youth of the world as God had commanded him. My wife's uncle John Bueno served as a missionary in El Salvador at the time. He organized churches and volunteers to deliver God's Word to every school, to every student. The *Book of Hope* was quickly put together as a Scripture book that told the life story of Jesus and led children to commit their lives to Him. And in an amazing miracle of rapid generosity, friends and supporters in the United States gave to print and ship nearly a million copies so that every teacher could also have one, in addition to every student.

Enthusiastic volunteers took the books in vans and buses, on bicycles and donkeys, and even carried boxes of books on their heads to get them to the schools and to the children. One teacher in a one-room schoolhouse far out in the rural countryside began to cry when the team arrived. She said no one ever remembered them because they were so far from any city! She was so grateful that she asked the volunteers to stay and explain the books to the children. They were able to share their own stories of transformation. In fact, in schools across the country the teachers and principals said, "You've come all this way with the book. Please stay and tell the children about it."

Of course local churches organized events for the children and their families to attend, and by God's grace, many young lives and their parents were miraculously touched and transformed. One event in particular comes to mind because I met her in 2007, as we celebrated OneHope's twentieth anniversary.

BLANCA

Sad. Lonely. Hungry. That was Blanca's story.

Her war-decimated homeland of El Salvador was a harsh place

in 1987, especially for children like Blanca, whose father had died and her mother was struggling to raise Blanca and her five siblings alone.

But God had a plan for Blanca's life. Someone placed a copy of that very first edition of the *Book of Hope* into her hands. Local churches and believers had taken the books across the nation into every school. Blanca was amazed by the joy she saw on the faces of the young people who came to her school with this precious gift for her.

"They would never be so happy if they had a life like mine," she thought. "Their lives must be perfect."

For years after she received the *Book of Hope,* she would read the book and wrestle with God: "If You are a loving God, why did You take my father? Why is our family trapped in such poverty? Why is there so much injustice?"

But then after ten years, suddenly the Holy Spirit, who always accompanies the Word, took hold in Blanca's life. She began to see that perhaps the kind of joy she'd seen in those young people *was* possible for her, despite the bleak circumstances.

"My life changed," she says, "because that seed remained planted in my heart."

Blanca chose to follow Christ as Savior. She went on planting that "seed" of the Word in others many times over. When she grew up and got married, her son read her Scripture book. Her daughter read it. Today every member of her family has accepted the message of salvation, and all are vibrant believers.

And the tattered *Book of Hope* she received more than twenty years ago is still one of Blanca's most treasured possessions.

"I give my sincerest thanks to the Lord Jesus Christ for the people who do the beautiful work of preaching the Word of God," she says today, referring to those who first sent God's Word to her. "I pray to the Lord for them, that they would always keep the fire in their hearts so that the ministry of the *Book of Hope* continues. For there are many souls who need to hear the good news of salvation, the blessed gospel of His Word, because that is how my testimony begins."

When Blanca tells her story, she also shares her incredible passion for the youth of this world, her understanding of how Satan wishes to destroy them, and how treacherous it is to "cross the terrible bridge of youth without Christ."

I hear what she's saying, and I marvel that more than twenty years after she first received her children's Scripture book, she still has it—the book *and* the passion.

DIMA

God's Word has power to affect destiny! We've seen it again and again, and not just in Latin America. The ministry of OneHope has expanded across Latin America, to Russia, India, and beyond. I'm reminded of a good friend and fellow minister Dima Teplyakov in Russia. Dima's father was an alcoholic. His grandfather had been an alcoholic. A huge segment of the Russian population of males has fallen victim to alcoholism—and Dima was next in line.

It was 1992. Dima's hometown of Krasnoyarsk in Siberia had been a "closed city" under Soviet rule. But as the Iron Curtain fell, it became wide open to *glasnost* and a host of outside influences. A predisposition to alcoholism may have been in his DNA, and he already ran with a crowd of vodka-swilling friends, but now Dima could investigate many other possible sources of addiction.

"I'd say 70 percent of my group of friends would use any kind of alcohol and drugs," says Dima, who was seventeen at the time. "It was very serious. We had no hopes, no direction."

Like most boys his age in Russia, Dima had thought very little about God. The only "godlike" person he could imagine was Lenin, who was revered, whose good name and good works had been "sold" to Russia's children for seventy years.

Then the Americans came to town.

"Our teacher at school told us that some Americans had come,"

Dima remembers. "We were so excited. It was like the circus came to town." He listened closely to all that these American Christians had to say. "They shared about their personal lives, how something bad could be changed to a better life."

The Americans were volunteers, members of various churches in the United States, who had heeded the call to come to this newly opened city in Siberia and put God's Word into the hands of Russian children. This was the first-ever large-scale distribution of God's Word in Krasnoyarsk. Because there were no local churches for OneHope to work with at the time, the ministry had made plans to launch a new church for anyone who came to Christ through this initial outreach.

Dima received his own copy of the *Book of Hope* from the team, took it home, and began to read it. He was amazed to read about the life of Christ, His miracles, His teachings, and even His death on the cross and joyful resurrection.

"This was my first experience of the Word of God," Dima says.

It was more powerful than he could have imagined. Soon Dima had committed his life to Christ, and he began to attend the new church that had been launched in Krasnoyarsk. Suddenly his old life—with the crowd of drinking and drugging teenagers—held no allure. Now he had found, in the person of Jesus Christ, a real purpose and hope for living.

Accepting Christ at a HopeFest Celebration and learning God's Word through the pages of the *Book of Hope* were only the beginning of a journey that has taken Dima to Bible school and then to Vladivostok, where he became a pastor and planted three churches!

It looked as if destiny had marked out a life of hopelessness and a descent into addiction for Dima, just like the other men in his family before him. But God had a very different plan. He had called out Dima to become a believer and a minister, and Dima is still pursuing that lifelong calling. By God's grace Dima's ministry continues to impact people in Russia, and he trains workers who have a passion for China in order to multiply that ministry.

Dima is radically determined to give everything to Christ, and he encourages others to do so as well.

His story perfectly portrays the power of a biblical message of purpose and hope, which OneHope is committed to presenting to the next generation. Each Scripture-engagement tool we develop embodies this message, because it is this hope that is so desperately needed by the next generation, as Dima's story shows.

RUSSIA

His story was a success story. In the Russian city of Beslan we were not so successful. Perhaps you remember the tragedy that unfolded there on the first day of school in September 2004. More than 1,100 students, teachers, and parents were held captive in a school gym by Islamic terrorists. It was reported that the captors gave the children some dried fruit to eat, knowing it would make them thirsty—then denied them water. By the end of their three days of hell on earth, the little ones were forced to drink their own urine.

In the midst of this horror some children from the local Sunday school understood that when you are faced with a living hell, there is only Jesus. They hurriedly wrote out scriptures such as the Lord's Prayer and secretly passed them on to their schoolmates to give them courage. Whenever they were allowed to, they lifted their little voices in songs from church.

"God is so good, God is so good..."

In the face of hell's worst God's children held their ground and praised the Lord.

I was in a plane on the way to Moscow the day Satan poured out his wrath upon Beslan, Russia, bringing the gym roof down on top of those children and the others who were trapped with them. When Russian authorities tried to end the standoff, there was a firefight with the terrorists. Terrified children, some naked and covered with blood, tried to flee through the carnage, but far too many didn't make it. A 2009 USA Today article reported that

333 people died that day, and more than half of these victims were children.[1]

I arrived in a different Moscow on September 3, 2004. I had flown into this same airport thirty-nine times before, and the procedure is always the same: you go through passport control, get your luggage, fill out a customs form, and go through customs. When you come out of customs, there is always a crowd of people you have to work your way through to find the person you are meeting. But that day as I came through customs, there was no jam-packed crowd. There were about three hundred people, looking up at a TV monitor in a bracket on the wall, and they were weeping and heartbroken.

I arrived in a nation that had been dramatically changed. Beslan was Russia's 9/11. The whole country was at a standstill. My meetings in Moscow were canceled. I was alone in my hotel room with nothing to do but weep and pray, and the Lord clearly told me to go to Beslan.

He said something to me then that I did not fully understand at the time: "Do you realize that I experience 9/11 every day? I see Beslan every day. I see My children go into eternity without knowledge of who I am."

That is hard for us to even imagine or comprehend. We live in the seen, the finite, and the temporal. God sees what suffering humanity will experience without Him. I prayed, "Lord, help me to try to see the world as You see it." Maybe that is impossible, but the Lord told me at that time to visit Beslan, and I would experience a little of what He experiences every time a lost soul goes into eternity without Him.

In Beslan I simply wept for days. With each new friend I made, I heard a new story of horror and tragedy.

One young mother had accompanied her proud six-year-old boy to school that day, carrying her infant child in her arms. The terrorists grew tired of hearing babies cry and commanded all mothers with babies to leave. The woman tried to leave with her baby and her little son, but they wouldn't allow it.

She could take her baby, but she must leave her son behind. Her little boy did not survive.

I went to the cemetery where there are more than three hundred graves of children. An old man wept by a grave where two bodies had been laid to rest side-by-side. He told me, "In these graves are my only daughter and my only grandchild."

For those few days I saw the world a little bit as Jesus sees it, heartbroken and stunned at the immensity of the tragedy. And a part of me cried out for revenge too. Surely such great evil should not go unanswered.

I wanted to take vengeance on someone. But who? This kind of evil didn't originate in the heart of man but in the heart of our enemy the devil. How can we take revenge on him? Yes, he would hate it if we foiled a terrorist plot and protected children like these from death, but I realized he hates it even worse when we reach those children with the gospel and save them from eternal death.

If we want our revenge on Satan, then what we need to do is bring children to Jesus. I made that pledge in the cemetery in Beslan. I told the devil: "I pledge to you that until I die, that in every town, village, and hamlet, the Word of the Lord will go forth and reach every child in the former Soviet Union. Hear me, enemy. What you intended for evil, the church through God's power will use for good."

I sometimes think the worst tragedies require the deepest healing and engender the most potent responses. Our partner pastors in Russia came together with me to form our response. At that time they had already used the *Book of Hope* to plant more than two thousand churches from 1991 to 2004. In 2004 alone they had established more than three hundred more faith communities.

"But it's not enough," Pastor Edward Grabovenko told me after the Beslan massacre. "We're not reaching the children fast enough."

From this tragedy was born the plan to send Bible school

students and graduates in small teams, traveling fast and light, with the *Book of Hope* and *The GodMan* film throughout Russia. They presented HopeFest Celebrations, showed the film, led children and families to Jesus, then organized "preaching points" or Bible studies that met once a week to disciple new believers until a church could be established. The program worked well and helped launch new churches. It was a good initial response to Beslan. But as I say, the toughest tragedies spur us to the greatest responses when we allow Christ's love to heal and guide.

The next tragedy involved our partner Bishop Artur Suleimanov of the Russian Pentecostal Union. He was martyred for his faith, gunned down by a radical Islamic extremist. He and others in his Hosanna House of Prayer in Dagestan, a traditionally Muslim region, had been receiving death threats demanding they close the church and leave town.

"In some regions of Russia, we may grumble about defamation articles labeling evangelicals as 'cults' or 'sects' and sometimes about the impossibility to rent a community center to do a crusade," Pastor Edward said. "But in Dagestan, on the other hand, people would be happy to have *those* problems. Shootings on religious grounds is common. You can be shot if you are a Christian bringing the good news of Christ. And killers don't stop when they succeed in killing one; they would try to blow up the cemetery where people would gather for the funeral of their friend, brother, sister, or loved one."

Pastor Edward attended the funeral for Bishop Artur. Because the assassination had been classified as a terror attack, the proceedings were guarded by armed soldiers. The mere sight of it brought home again to him that Christians in Islamic regions of Russia are truly on the battlefront.

"I admire the church in Dagestan for their courage and their resolute decision to follow God no matter what happens," Pastor Edward said. His final lines in the report he sent me were very eloquent about the mission in Russia (and around the world):

Bishop Artur's wife will continue to share Christ's good news where Artur cannot take it now. And such was also the desire of the church—to continue to reach out with the gospel. And so should we. And may the memory of dedicated saints stir in us the desire and the courage to go all the way—and, as we finish our race, to be taken into the kingdom of the One who is the Alpha and the Omega, the First and the Last, the victorious King of kings, Jesus Himself. But now, we still have work to do.

Indeed we do. From this tragedy a new and powerful ministry outreach was formed. Pastor Edward went on to be elected to lead the Pentecostal Union in Russia. He and I together sought God and received from the Lord an amazing vision for completing what I had vowed in Beslan—to reach every child and youth in Russia with God's life-transforming Word. In honor of our friend Bishop Artur, Edward led his fellowship in launching the "Hosanna Plan" (named for Bishop Artur's church). It's similar to the Beslan Project but on a much broader scale. It's a plan to present the gospel in the approximately 100,000 towns and villages of Russia that have still had *no* gospel witness in the twenty years since the fall of the Iron Curtain. Local believers are asked to give one year of their lives to become missionaries to their own country, and many hundreds have already responded to the call.

By the year 2020 the Hosanna Plan will have touched the lives of one hundred million people with the gospel. At least one million are expected to come to faith in Christ, and ten thousand churches will be planted. What Satan intended for evil—in the slaughter at Beslan and the martyrdom of a friend and partner—God will use for good and the salvation of many.

It thrills my soul that OneHope and I are part of this amazing Hosanna Plan for Russia. This nation is dear to my heart, as I've been deeply involved in outreach there for many years. Kim and

I feel such a kinship with the Russian people, we even named our younger daughter Natasha, a common name for Russian girls.

The lesson we learned through tragedy and triumph in Russia is this: the greatest expression of our "affect destiny" mission can be born out of the deepest pain. It's the same way that a crucifixion was necessary to bring eternal hope—to transform sin and death into life and liberty. The same way my blindness and year of struggle were necessary to transform my life and ministry. What has been your Beslan, your blindness, your darkest hour? Have you allowed God to transform it into the victory and calling that He intends for you?

I encourage you not to waste a single heartache but to seek for God's plan in the middle of it. He doesn't let us suffer needlessly, and your suffering may be the bridge to your destiny.

Chapter 7

THE SILENT REVOLUTION

ONE HUNDRED MILLION people are set to be reached before the year 2020 in Russia. In India 129,093,199 have already been reached. Approaching one billion all across the globe. The OneHope numbers are almost shocking when it comes to how many children and youth we're impacting with God's Word all around the world. And we have a plan to achieve mission fulfillment—providing a relevant presentation of the gospel to *every* boy and girl on earth—by the year 2030. It's extraordinary, and we give God praise for what He has done!

And yet if you ask most evangelical Christians in the United States what they know about OneHope's mission to the next generation, the most common answer is a blank stare. Dr. Charles Osueke, the General Superintendent of the Assemblies of God in Nigeria, saw how, by God's grace, OneHope was transforming young lives in his nation—and across Africa—and declared it a "silent revolution."

It's a silent revolution of believers who know that the Great Commission is doable and who want to be part of it. It's made up of people like you and me who are in pursuit of touching one billion young lives with God's love and His Word, and then the next billion, and then every generation until Christ returns!

How did we get here? My dad received the vision, as you know. But he didn't have millions of dollars to invest in it. And we don't have any celebrity supporters or endorsements. Here's what we had (as you'll remember from chapter 5): God's direction to obey, trust, and have faith—the same directions you have from God in your everyday life.

Jesus gave those directions to me in a personal way at the moment I most needed to hear them, but my dad had already been acting on them all his life. The lesson of obey that Christ spoke into my heart was the lesson of "just go!" that my dad had been teaching me for years. Remember the story of how he went to British Guyana with $5.68 in his pocket and a one-way ticket? He told that to me many times, always saying, "When God tells you to go, *just go*. When God speaks, just do what He says." My dad always trusted God to provide, and he always went where God told him to go. After I began to learn this lesson, extraordinary things happened to me too.

I remember flying home from a long trip in Russia. I was on the seven-hour flight from Siberia to Moscow, perfectly exhausted and so ready to catch my flight home from Moscow to see my wife and daughter. (Natasha wasn't born yet.)

The Russian gentleman next to me on the flight spoke very good English. He was reading a newspaper, so I asked him what was in the news. This was before the fall of the USSR. Gorbachev was still in power, but things were really stirred up; there were riots, strikes, financial crisis, and a great move toward throwing off the chains of communism. These were exciting times!

My seatmate on the plane began to tell me that at that moment in the Siberian town of Kemerovo the coal miners were on strike. Up until very recently the idea of a strike was unheard of in Russia. Because of the importance of the coal industry in Kemerovo this strike was getting a lot of attention. In fact, there was speculation it might touch off what would become known as the "Second Russian Revolution" and play a part in bringing down the USSR.

As we talked, I began to hear the Lord's leading, and He was saying, "Kemerovo. Go to Kemerovo." Nothing could have been lower on my wish list than to go to Kemerovo. It was back in Siberia, the complete opposite direction from where I wanted to go. I told the Lord, "I want to see my wife and daughter. I've been gone too much as it is." But the only reply I received was this: Kemerovo.

When the plane landed in Moscow, a Russian pastor had come to meet me and help me get from the domestic airport to the international airport for my flight home. He was dumbfounded when I asked, "Can I get to Kemerovo from here tonight?" He said, "Kemerovo is in Siberia. You just came from Siberia."

I said, "I know it sounds crazy, but the Lord has told me to go to Kemerovo."

We found out that there was only one flight to Kemerovo that night, and it was oversold. I was so happy! There was no way I, along with my interpreter, could get on an oversold flight. Just so God could see I was trying to be obedient, I put our names on the standby list, knowing that we would never be able to go—until at the last moment, one seat cleared.

If I went, I would go alone, with no interpreter, to a Russian city I'd never been to, hours in the wrong direction from the one place I wanted to be.

I went. I wasn't happy about it, but I went.

About six o'clock the next morning I arrived in Kemerovo, a city of seven hundred thousand people, where I knew not a single soul; a city in chaos because of the labor strikes, where I could only communicate through hand gestures. If you know anything about the Russian language, you know there's no such thing as knowing "enough Russian to get by." I managed to get to a hotel, drop to my knees before God, and say, "I'm here with no idea what I'm doing here. Now what?"

After I prayed and interceded for the city of Kemerovo, I thought maybe that was all I had to do—pray. Maybe God had called me here just to pray for Kemerovo. But then God spoke to me again and told me to go to the university and find someone who speaks English. God led me to a student named Julie who wanted to practice her English. She took me to see the mayor of Kemerovo and helped me talk to him about Jesus and the *Book of Hope*. Three months later I came back to that city with a team of ministry volunteers and the *Book of Hope* for every student in the city.

During that ministry event sixteen thousand boys and girls signed decision cards saying they wanted to follow Jesus. We were able to leave a great missionary couple in Kemerovo to begin a new church, and a wonderful work was born.

Ilia

A few years later I met a young man from Kemerovo named Ilia. He said he wanted to thank me for bringing the *Book of Hope*, because the book led him to the Lord eight years previously when he received it in school.

He said, "I don't know if you know what has been happening with the church in Kemerovo since then. A bunch of us at the university realized nobody had taken the *Book of Hope* to the city of Novokuznetsk, so we did a distribution there, and we helped a church plant, which has about eight hundred members now."

Further, he told me, the believers at Novokuznetsk were worried about the Altai people in the mountains beyond them, because they had never heard of Jesus. So these new believers in Novokuznetsk took the *Book of Hope* to the Altai people.

According to the Joshua Project, they are listed among the most unreached people groups of the world. But that is going to have to change, because there are now thirty-six Christians among those Buddhist Altai!

Yes, I have learned from my dad's simple wisdom and the leading of the Savior that when God says to go, just go. Obey Him. Trust Him. This has been the way OneHope has grown and the way God has stretched my faith again and again. But remember, there was a second direction in the word the Lord gave to me in the midst of my blindness: trust.

We've had to confront this one many times when what God asked seemed impossible.

"What Can You Believe Me For?"

The moment is so clear in my mind. I had been on staff with OneHope for a few years, and the forward progression seemed to have stalled out. We were reaching about six million children per year with God's Word. It was a great number, but God had told us to reach *every child and youth on earth*. Six million a year wouldn't do it; too many were moving into adulthood without ever hearing the good news of the gospel.

My dad and I were seeking the Lord in prayer. Why is this happening? How can we reach every child if You're only providing for six million a year?

We both felt so clearly the Lord's response, "What can you believe Me for?"

It wasn't that He was unable to provide for more than six million a year; it was that we weren't believing big enough. A spirit of wisdom and revelation seemed to come upon us, and we knew that what God wanted was to double the ministry output the following year. Can you imagine in business, with no promise of extra resources, if you just declared you were going to double your profits? It would be crazy. But we knew that God's power was working in us and through us, and we made a power declaration that the following year the ministry would present the good news to twelve million children and youth.

We made the declaration. We had no idea how it was going to happen. We were obedient to God's call and trusted Him as we made the plan that He impressed on our hearts. This is where that third direction, to *have faith*, came into play. Faith is truly the substance of things hoped for and the evidence of things not seen. Dad and I began to act on our belief, completely in faith. We made plans for a bigger building and the new staff we'd need when we doubled our faith goal. We started researching and dreaming about the new countries that we felt would open to the *Book of Hope*.

The first thing that happened: my faith was tested.

A missionary in the Philippines called me and said he'd heard of our program and needed me to come with him to meet the minister of education. He thought there was a good chance we'd get permission to give the *Book of Hope* to every schoolchild in the entire nation there. As he was speaking, a spirit of fear gripped me. Here was one of those doors opening, and we didn't have the money! This wasn't in the projections we'd made, and I didn't see how we could possibly do it. I called my dad right away.

"I have an invitation to meet with the minister of education in the Philippines, but looking at the numbers, I just don't see how we can add anything to our plate right now," I told him. I needed him to agree with me that it would be senseless to go to the Philippines.

There was silence at the other end of the line, and finally Dad said, "Who are you to say no to God?"

Ouch. Thanks, Dad.

I got on a plane for Manila.

The meeting with the minister of education was extraordinary. He was not a believer, but he was so gracious and listened to my presentation and then complimented the United States for all we had done for the Philippines after World War II to help build schools and create the system of education. But he said in 1963 when the United States removed Bibles from the classroom, the Philippines had done the same, and it was as a reflection of our own American laws that he had to, at that moment, deny me permission to take the Scriptures into the schools.

What a heartbreaking moment!

I immediately began to tell him how the United States had changed since prayer and the Bible were taken out of the schools, listing the statistics about drug use, alcoholism, teen pregnancy, and gang violence. Did he want this for the Philippines as well? It was already happening, he told me, and he began to list for me his country's statistics, which were the same or worse than mine.

I could almost pinpoint the very moment in our conversation when the Holy Spirit came over that nonbeliever, and he pushed back from his desk saying, "I don't even know why I'm doing this." He called his secretary in and dictated a letter granting us permission to give the *Book of Hope* to every single schoolchild in the nation. I was just praising God in my heart!

Then the man turned to me and said, "I'm putting my name, reputation, and seal on this letter, which will go to every school in the Philippines. Can you do this?"

Everything in my humanity said, "There's no way we can do this." The money wasn't there. The infrastructure wasn't in place. But again this was where those directions to trust, obey, and have faith were at work. Faith rose up in my spirit, and I said, "Yes, sir, we can do it." I couldn't do it, but I knew I was serving an almighty God who can do anything.

I boarded the plane for home, and on a layover in Japan I called my dad.

"I've got good news and bad news," I told him. "The good news is we have permission to reach 7.2 million schoolchildren in the Philippines. The bad news is we need two million dollars really bad." On the other end of the line I heard Dad chuckle. He began to explain.

At the same time we were grappling with financial issues, God had been speaking to a wonderful Christian businessman, Mr. Green. This man had a vision to reach the world with the gospel of Jesus, and he was seeking God's direction for how to do it. God had already made clear to him that there was a divine plan and that it would be revealed. In May of 1997 he and his family "just happened" to visit a church where a *Book of Hope* presentation was being made. When he heard about an economical way to blanket entire cities with the Word, he knew this could be the plan the Holy Spirit had promised to reveal to him!

Mr. Green had called my dad and asked him to come visit with him and his family. Of course my dad's schedule is planned well in advance, and the best he could do was promise to meet them next time he was in their area. Mr. Green wasn't satisfied with that. He asked Dad just to pray about it. And when Dad prayed about it, he felt the Holy Spirit's leading him to go and meet the Green family.

He was so glad he did. The Greens became one of our most generous partners. As I spoke to Dad about the Philippines that day, he said, "Rob, we have a gift of $500,000 and a commitment that will provide what we need for the outreach in the Philippines."

Together with the extraordinary generosity of many other friends, the Greens helped enable the ministry to more than double our outreach at the time.

Have faith. Obey, trust, and have faith.

This is how the scope and vision of the ministry of OneHope have grown. It has been a silent revolution, almost a secret from the rest of the evangelical church (although we don't try to keep it that way). But every day someone like you hears for the first time about OneHope and understands that they can make a powerful difference just by praying and giving, that they can help needy children move from death to life with such a simple gift—the gift of God's life-transforming Word—and feel called to make it happen. Then that person joins the silent revolution. They obey God, they trust Him, and they step out in faith, just as I did, my dad did, and the Green family did. Together we're turning the tables on the devil and rescuing the next generation by giving them the eternal hope of Jesus Christ.

Close to a billion children and young people have been touched by the gospel through obedience, trust, and faith in God. We're amazed every day to see the new directions He takes us and behold the astounding provision He makes for us. Millions in Russia, in India, and in Latin America—this silent revolution of believers who are willing to obey, trust, and put their faith in action are bringing hope to a generation!

We're affecting destiny, fulfilling the mission God put in our hearts.

And you? Are you part of this silent revolution? Are you affecting destiny for the generations to follow, for your own generation? Are you teaching your children and grandchildren how they can affect destiny?

You can do it, you know. Seek God for your own destiny, obey when He directs you, trust Him to make the path clear, and have faith that your own personal ministry will make the impact He desires.

TSENKO AND MATIU

I think about an American woman named Charlotte in Bulgaria. How many people do you know who've been to Bulgaria? It's not a tourist spot, by most standards. And Charlotte wasn't a tourist. She was a missionary. She'd followed her destiny and joined a short-term OneHope mission team (at that time we called them Affect Destiny Teams) to help present children and youth with God's Word. She was no Billy Graham. She was not even a Rob Hoskins. She couldn't speak the language, but she was part of the silent revolution, and by God's grace her impact has been felt in so many lives.

She was working with a team from the local church. One day they went to an orphanage. It was there Charlotte met Tsenko, an abandoned boy. His father had never been around very much. Tsenko could just remember him: a gambler who had a job but lost most of his money in various games of chance. When he disappeared, it was just after Tsenko's baby brother, Matiu, had been born. Their mom had no hope to provide for the boys. There was no work for a single mother in their rural part of Bulgaria. She went to Greece to find a job. She left baby Matiu with his grandparents and dropped Tsenko at the orphanage. Just a few years later Matiu joined him there. They were all alone.

Matiu didn't miss their father. He didn't remember him. But both boys missed their mother and their grandparents. The state made sure they had food and went to school, but boys need more than that. They need someone to comb their hair and help with their homework, to read to them and hug them and love them. Tsenko tried to be strong for Matiu, but he was lonely and felt hopeless.

The church team that came to visit brought a gift for each child, the Bulgarian language *Book of Hope*. They also organized a film showing to entertain the children. They presented *The GodMan*, seen through the eyes of a young boy who might have walked the streets of Jerusalem with Jesus.

Both fourteen-year-old Tsenko and ten-year-old Matiu enjoyed the film. Then when one of the people from the church began to explain to them that Jesus is real and that He is still loving and embracing children and adults today, Tsenko drew back. How could this be real?

The walls went up. But Charlotte was there, and she saw past those walls. As an interpreter helped her talk to Tsenko about his life and about what they'd seen in the film, he opened up to her. As she shared with him from the pages of the *Book of Hope*, things began to fall into place. Tsenko realized that Charlotte *believed*. And he promised her he would read the book, and he would try to believe too.

In the weeks that followed, Tsenko kept his promise to read the *Book of Hope*. It contained not only the scriptural story of Jesus but also special sections designed to speak to the heartfelt needs of young people like him. Slowly he began to realize that although he may not be able to live with his biological family, he could still have the unconditional love of a heavenly Father. Today Tsenko, Matiu, and thirty children from the orphanage are part of their local church, serving Jesus and worshipping together. The church even sends a Bible teacher to the orphanage to meet with them and pray with the young people each week.

Charlotte trusted God, obeyed His calling, and had faith that He would use her faithfulness to affect destiny. And it did, especially for Tsenko.

Be part of the silent revolution. Let God use you too to affect destiny for the next generation!

Chapter 8

SO WHAT?

S O IT'S A silent revolution that has presented the gospel to a worldwide total approaching one billion in more than one hundred twenty-five nations around the world. Millions in Russia, India, and Latin America, and yet what difference does it make?

So you give God's Word to a million children in, say, Swaziland. Um, so what?

What proof did we have other than stories like Tsenko's that our ministry was actually fulfilling the mission to affect destiny?

Back in those early days of our OneHope ministry, "success" was measured by output: how many people were reached, how many children received a book. Because I know the power of God's Word, I know that it will always make an impact wherever it is received. God Himself promises, "...so is my word that goes out from my mouth: It will not return to me empty, but will accomplish what I desire and achieve the purpose for which I sent it" (Isa. 55:11). It will always do what God intends.

NASSI

I had grown up hearing the stories of how even a scrap of a Bible page could bring someone to salvation. A Muslim boy named Nassi picked up some cheese from a street vendor one day, to find it wrapped in a page of the Bible. There was a paper shortage in

Tehran, Iran, at the time, and the merchant was using whatever he could find to wrap his customers' purchases. His father warned him against reading it, but Nassi read the page several times and the next day returned to the vendor to ask about the mysterious page. The merchant told him if he made another purchase, there was more such "wrapping paper" available. So he bought some figs, and the next day some dates, and then more cheese. Finally he had several pages of the Bible, each of which he had read again and again. But it was frustrating, because he was only receiving disjointed scraps of Scripture. From just these few pages he could tell there was a compelling message, and he longed to know what it was!

Motivated by what he had read in the throwaway scraps of the Word, he went searching for a Farsi-language Bible. He began to read it, and in just a few weeks he had chosen to become a follower of Christ.

WITCH DOCTOR LEADS A REMOTE TRIBE TO SALVATION

I heard of a missionary in Laos, during the final days of the French involvement there. He had been trying to discover a way to get up into the mountains and share the gospel with a certain tribe, but he was running out of time when he happened to meet some of these very tribesmen on the street of the city where he lived. They were visiting and didn't speak much French, but somehow he convinced them to come to his home for dinner. Before they left, he gave them a French-language New Testament and some other gospel literature. He doubted anyone in their village could read French, but it was all he had.

As it turned out, incredibly there was *one person* in the village who could read French: the witch doctor. He had learned to speak and read it in a government school.

Seven years later during a truce between the French and the

Laotian insurgents, the missionary was able to return to Laos and actually go to the mountainous region where he had always wanted to share the gospel with the tribes. He traveled for three days by train and horseback to the remote area. What he discovered there astonished him. In eleven remote villages the gospel had been preached, and there were 748 Christians in this tribe! The witch doctor who originally read the New Testament and gospel tracts had given his life to Christ. Because he was a respected elder, when he shared the message of salvation with others, they followed him in following Jesus! Every adult in his village had chosen Christ as Savior; then they had begun going to neighboring villages, sharing the good news.

God's Word makes a difference, wherever and however you present it to people!

AND THE LORD SAID...

I remember the story my father told years ago of a South American gentleman who received a little gospel booklet from some Christian young people on the street corner one day as he hurried home from work. When he saw it was a booklet about God, he ripped it up and threw it away. At some point he had decided he hated God, the church, and anyone representing the church. (Quite possibly his antagonism had been exacerbated by the Marxist literature that was flooding Latin America at the time.)

But when he arrived home that night, he found a scrap of the booklet still clinging to the sleeve of his shirt. He brushed it off but couldn't help seeing what was written on it: "And the Lord said..." He threw the scrap of paper away with a curse. But he couldn't get the phrase out of his head. "And the Lord said..."

All through dinner he thought about it. He didn't even sleep well that night because it kept echoing in his dreams. "And the Lord said..."

The next day at work the phrase still dogged his thoughts. As he hurried home again that evening, he was overjoyed to see the same team of young people on the same street corner, handing out the same booklets. He rushed up to one of the young men, and said, "Please, please tell me what the Lord said!"

He listened to the gospel message, dedicated his life to Christ, and later became a pastor.

This is the power of the living Word to transform lives, even if only a tiny scrap of it is read. I believe with all my heart that it's the Holy Spirit who speaks to people through the Word, and He can do His miraculous work in astounding ways. We can't be the Holy Spirit. We can't convict anyone of their sins and draw them to repentance. All we can do is point the way. How do we do this best and most effectively? Coming from a publishing background because of my father's ministry, of course I had gravitated toward God's Word as a book placed in the hands of a child, who would receive individual ownership of it.

As doors opened to reach various countries and cultures, I could not help but be influenced by my in-laws, the Buenos, and their remarkable media ministry. The leadership team of OneHope began to pray and discuss exactly what we meant by God's Word in our mission statement: *to affect destiny by providing God's eternal Word to all the children and youth of the world.* Our mission *had been* to get a book into the hands of a child. But through the development of *The GodMan* film we'd come to see that a visual presentation of the gospel, received collectively rather than individually, could still be called "God's Word" and could still have a powerful, life-transformational impact.

At the same time it became very real to me that in many cases the church had lost its ability to speak prophetically to our world. "Church" had somehow come to be seen as old-fashioned and irrelevant. We have a timeless message to share, but it is also a message that must interact with place and time or it *does* become irrelevant. You see, Jesus Christ—the Savior of mankind—spoke with a prophetic voice, tailoring His message to first-century Jews in a way that still allows it to be accessible to us today. Much of the way evangelicals were talking to twenty-first-century unchurched people was all but incomprehensible to them because they *were* twenty-first-century unchurched people and the church was still speaking nineteenth- and twentieth-century "Christianese."

Good pastors, of course, know how to speak with a prophetic voice in a way that makes itself heard. Every week a good pastor uses the Scriptures to meet the needs of his congregation. He takes stock of their lives and issues, he looks in the Scriptures for the answers to their most urgent questions, and he interprets God's Word, through exegesis, in a way that his people can receive and incorporate it in their own lives. For a while now OneHope has been involved in a conversation on how to do this exegesis, not for a congregation but for a generation, for a nation, for a culture. We were looking for our unifying, prophetic message that would touch and transform.

In fact, we were formulating an answer to that question, "What constitutes God's Word?" We found it could come in the form of a video, a text message, a website, or a rave. (Yes! Our *True Love* multimedia presentation was designed to share God's love through music, text, and visuals at dance clubs and parties.) We were grappling with questions of how to do proper exegesis for certain segments of the population within their culture and demographics.

Then a new question was thrown into the mix. This question was "So what?"

So what if you are giving God's Word to more than a million children in Russia every year? So what if you presented *The GodMan* film to seven million young people in India through one massive nationwide outreach? So what if you have carte blanche to take the *Book of Hope* into the schools of Swaziland? *So what?*

It wasn't me asking the question. It was God. And it was in Swaziland that He asked it.

Swaziland

Swaziland is a tiny landlocked African country. Its economy is very dependent upon that of its larger neighbor, South Africa. Swaziland is a kingdom, the only country I'm aware of that has remained a functioning monarchy for centuries, never under the control of any colonial power or any other country. And it's supposedly a Christian nation: 80 percent of the population claims to follow Jesus Christ.[1] Every year the king goes on national television and preaches to the people about the gospel and the nation's Christian heritage. Visit Swaziland, and everywhere you'll see expressions of the faith: billboards, bumper stickers, and advertising.

Yet Swaziland is slated to be the first nation ever in which the entire population will simply go extinct, according to UN prognostications, because of HIV/AIDS.[2] The average life expectancy of a Swazi citizen is only thirty-two years.

How can we reconcile such a high rate of HIV with a Christian nation? I'll tell you: because the forms of Christianity took hold but the underlying biblical worldview did not. And when Western civilization came pouring into Swaziland through the global media, the "forms" of Christianity weren't enough to protect the next generation.

Let me tell you about my visit to Swaziland in 2005. We wanted to document how our Scripture-engagement tools were making a difference. We wanted to gauge, as best we could, the effectiveness of our outreach in impacting the next generation. I have to admit that I was going there because on paper this appeared to be one of our role model programs. We had permission from the government to be in every school. We had praying teachers teaching our curriculum, churches assigned for follow-up in the schools, and we were reaching tens of thousands of children a month. Little did I suspect that the program I had come to showcase would really open my eyes to a stark prophetic reality.

When we arrived at the Swaziland airport, there was a television mounted on a wall bracket, right there in the hall of arrivals, and a very racy music video with a barely dressed female rapper was blaring. The lyrics were even more jarring and obscene. The pastors and missionaries who met us seemed oblivious, or had grown immune, to the lunacy of soft porn in a public venue of a nation literally dying from sexual dysfunction.

Our host for this visit was a former businessman who had gone into full-time ministry after a heart-wrenching experience: he and his wife had rescued a street child who had been beaten, sodomized, and left for dead. This horror graphically illuminated for them just how desperately the children of Swaziland needed help and protection. He showed me a local newspaper that clearly illustrated the worst problems facing his country's next generation. The headline read: "Four students raped by teacher." Welcome to Swaziland.

This theme of sexual abuse of children was driven home to me many times during our stay. I met a twelve-year-old girl who had a hard decision to make: she could sleep with her school bus driver once a month or walk the six kilometers to school and six kilometers back home every day. I discovered that schoolteachers were the people most likely to sexually abuse the children. I met a twenty-four-year-old teacher and confronted him with this statistic, and he became angry, demanding to know if I owned a house and a car. When I admitted I did, he said, "I don't have a car or a house. The only thing I have to give me pleasure is these young girls in my classroom. Who are you to tell me I can't have them?" Something had gone drastically wrong; something had convinced him that because he could not have the wealth of a middle-class westerner, he was entitled to the "comfort" he could get from raping his students.

Our ministry chairman also shared this story with me, about the time during a trip when members of our team stopped at a gas station in the rural north and a beautiful little girl came up to him, said hello, and made a simple offer: "If you give me two dollars, sir, you can have me."

We have a photograph of this little girl. She was a lovely child, and she was wearing a pretty, red sweater. Whenever we shared this story, whenever we thought about Swaziland, we could not help but refer to "the girl in the red sweater." She exemplified what had gone wrong in Swaziland and what had gone wrong with our OneHope ministry there.

Her story helps illuminate how a supposedly Christian nation also became the nation with the highest AIDS rate in the world. The true life of Jesus Christ had not been transmitted to the next generation. The scriptural worldview that should have given adults the foundation to protect and nurture children had never taken root. The onslaught of globalization, with its constant emphasis on self and pleasure, washed away any power the traditions of Christianity once had to change lives, and this left Swaziland's most vulnerable people open to horrific abuse. Our host told us no less than one in three children experienced some form of sexual abuse.

At that time we were working with churches in Swaziland, delivering God's Word to the children.

I shut it down.

I didn't want to be part of the enabling culture of Christianity that until then had no transforming power to change the lives of these children. We had been given permission to distribute God's Word freely in all the schools, but knowing that it might be handed out by the very person who would later sexually abuse the children who received it—we couldn't be part of that.

God's Word was reaching the next generation, and they were still dying in their sin. Thousands of schoolchildren were receiving the *Book of Hope*, and so what?

It was making little or no difference at all.

Chapter 9

AFFECT DESTINY—WHAT
DOES IT MEAN?

W HAT IS TRANSFORMATION? What does it mean to affect destiny? These questions forced themselves into my consciousness in Swaziland, but as I explained in chapter 8, the OneHope leadership team had already been grappling with similar puzzles for the few years previous to that experience.

We had discovered that God's Word could come in any medium that clearly represented the gospel and opened hearts to receive salvation and become transformed by His power. Our Scripture-engagement tools still relied primarily on Scripture, but the presentations varied widely. We had discovered that one pressing need was to speak a unified, prophetic message that clearly illuminated the salvation story. This was a critical component of the Word of God. It was not our intent to give a Bible to a child and say, "All the answers are in there! Have at it." Our expression among ourselves was, "We don't want to give them a bag of groceries. We want to give them a meal." Our message had to be compelling and clear for the target audience.

Of course this is what I thought, hoped, and prayed we'd produced for Swaziland, but it just wasn't working. This visit to Swaziland, my conversation with the schoolteacher, and the incident with the girl in the red sweater all coalesced to cause us to begin grappling with these questions: Is it enough to give God's Word? How do you ensure you're doing effective ministry to children and youth?

Our heartbeat was to engage every young person with the gospel in a meaningful way, and somehow it was faltering. I didn't know how to make it better or even how to gauge how badly off it might be. You do this same kind of "health check" on a church in the United States, and the reports are almost always couched in numbers: "We're doing great! We had twenty-five hundred people at our Easter program, and our children's church has seven hundred fifty kids every Sunday!" Or perhaps, "Not so good. There were only fifty people at our last midweek service, and we had to combine the elementary and junior high Sunday school classes because there aren't enough kids."

The numbers seem to be the standard of how well or how poorly the actual mission is being achieved. But I'd learned in Swaziland that the numbers just don't tell the truth all the time. The numbers don't tell whether lives are being transformed, whether we are truly affecting destiny, which is our ultimate mission.

My heart was torn. How could I know whether transformation was really taking place? How could I measure whether destiny had been affected? How could we have prevented a Swaziland situation? I didn't know, but I needed to find out.

That's why I thank the Lord for the people He has brought together with Dad and me to lead and shape the ministry of OneHope. Our team is amazing. So often I've reflected on Christ's command to pray to the Lord of the harvest for workers. The right people in place, with hearts open to the Holy Spirit's leading, make all the difference. One of these talented and dedicated OneHope workers is Chad Causey, our vice president of Global Ministries. He became my partner in searching for the answers.

He and I both knew very well that God's Word is God's Word, and it's the Holy Spirit who directs response, not us. In 1 Corinthians 3:5–6 Paul answered believers who were attributing their salvation to one apostle or another, "Who then is Paul, and who is Apollos, but ministers through whom you believed, as the Lord gave to each one? I planted, Apollos watered, but God gave the increase" (NKJV). We have a role to play, but it is God who gives the increase. Our desire then is for the increase, for fruitfulness, as the Bible instructs.

When you examine the teachings of Christ, when you look throughout the Bible, actually, you see this aspect of being fruitful again and again. Jesus speaks of a sower and seeds, a vineyard and vintner, and a fig tree and figs. In the passage from above Paul addresses planting and watering. Proverbs speaks of the difference between the fruitfulness of a lazy man and an industrious one. It's clear in Scripture that an important criterion for faithfulness is *fruitfulness*. Jesus even prayed His last night on earth before the crucifixion that we, His disciples, would bear much fruit—fruit that lasts.

Chad and I shared with the OneHope team the instinctive knowledge that *we* cannot change anyone, *we* cannot bring about transformation, but we *can* do our work in the best possible and most effective manner for bringing about the lasting fruit of changed lives. This was our biblical model: What would result in the most fruitful ministry? The fruit we desired to see was changed lives, transformation, and destiny affected. The methods we wanted to use were those that would bring about the most fruit.

Jesus said, "I am the true vine, and My Father is the vinedresser. Every branch in Me that does not bear fruit He takes away; and every branch that bears fruit He prunes, that it may bear more fruit" (John 15:1–2, NKJV). This became our plan: evaluate programs for their fruitfulness, enhance the ones that were bearing fruit, try to fix the ones that weren't, and, if necessary, end those that could not be made fruitful.

We were pursuing fruitfulness. The move was being made from measuring success by "outputs" (how many we could reach) to measuring success by "outcomes" (the resulting life-transformation among those we reached). The first hurdle, then, was that of measuring the success. How can we know if a life has been transformed by God's Word if we don't know what that life was like *before* the encounter with God's Word? We assembled a team of gifted researchers to help answer this.

We launched our Spiritual State of the World's Children research project with the help of local churches, ministries, and educators in nation after nation. We've completed the research in forty-four nations. The information we've cultivated has proved invaluable and has made it possible for us to determine whether a specific Scripture-engagement program is achieving its desired outcomes.

Our quest to answer the questions "What is the Word of God?" and "What does it mean to affect destiny?" has resulted in the new four pillars of OneHope ministry.

1. A unified, prophetic message. This is what every Scripture tool we create must present in a way that speaks to the target audience in the context of their lived reality and experience.

2. Research-based products. In the past we created a *Book of Hope* in the language of the children we wanted to reach. Now we interact with partners, take into account the research, and create a tool and program most likely to speak to the specific issues of our target audience in their age group and their culture. (The practical upshot of this is that we used to create up to five global programs per year. Now we create dozens, based on specific needs among specific demographics in specific cultures.)

3. Outcome-based programs. With the research tools now available to us, we're able to create products and programs that can be evaluated on their outcomes as they're developed and as they're rolled out for initial

distribution. Each new program is developed, pilot-tested, evaluated, rolled out, and then tested again to make sure the pilot-test results are holding true. All efforts are directed toward increasing fruitfulness.

4. Partner-driven ministry. Our partnerships with local churches and ministry organizations are the backbone of OneHope's frontline ministry. And while we do have OneHope teams that go out and do specific jobs, far and away the majority of our Scripture-engagement tools are used by local ministries to fulfill their calling and vision.

This idea of partner-driven ministry in itself has made OneHope the true servant of the national church and local missions organizations worldwide. We began sharing the results of our research with other organizations and churches right away, and local Christian leaders were the ones who later helped us evaluate it and discover what the correct responses were.

To this day I still remember my conversation with two Christian leaders in Malawi. They'd heard about the *Book of Hope,* and they were ready to do school distributions or whatever we asked. They were anxious to reach Malawi's next generation with the gospel. I think they were surprised when I told them, "I want you to tell me what your vision is, what God is calling you to do. Then we'll explore how meaningful Scripture engagement among Malawi's children and youth can drive the vision. And OneHope may be able to create Scripture tools to help you do *better* what God has already called you to do." But this is how we view the ministry of OneHope, as the helper and supporter of the local church and local ministries.

The Spiritual State of the World's Children research and our other custom discovery research projects have also helped unite us with our partners and unite local churches with each other in life-transforming ministry. Where the previous model had been to come in with our product and get local churches to help us distribute it, we're now able to give to our local partners tools they've specifically requested based on what the research shows them is needed. And while local partners may not all be united under one outreach banner, they are all working toward the same, unified outcome. Affected destiny equals transformed lives!

I believe this with all my heart: To know the future of a nation, you must know the state of its children. And I'd like to share a little bit of our research results with you here, because I think you might find it shocking. And I think it will help you understand the challenges we're facing in presenting the Word of God to the next generation. We found:

- In Peru 84 percent of young people say they are Christians, but 70 percent of young people are not sure or do not believe that the soul is eternal and survives beyond the body.

- In South Africa 84 percent say they've made a personal commitment to Jesus, but yet 53 percent do not believe in the physical resurrection of Christ.

- In the United States 72 percent say forgiveness of sins is only possible through Jesus Christ, but yet 57 percent still believe all "good people" earn a spot in heaven.

Clearly there are great segments of the youth population who believe mutually contradictory things about the nature of Jesus, Christianity, salvation, and eternity. These contradictions become even more glaring in many nations of Africa, where Christian missionaries have ministered for two hundred years, yet somehow the postmodern message of moral relativism has taken root. For instance, in the nation of Malawi:

- Eighty-nine percent of children and youth said they had made a personal commitment to Jesus Christ, and yet 54 percent denied the physical resurrection of Christ.

- Ninety-two percent said Jesus was born to a virgin, but 83 percent said that Jesus was not a real person.

- Eighty-four percent said forgiveness of sins is only possible through faith in Jesus Christ, but 75 percent still believe all religions pray to the same God.

- Ninety-two percent said a close relationship with God is important to them, but 90 percent also said they do not believe or are not sure if God exists.

The numbers don't make any sense, unless we allow that huge segments of Malawi's next generation are able to believe two mutually exclusive things or that they simply do not understand what Christianity is, who Christ is, or how the plan of salvation actually works.

For these children and youth to receive a truly *biblical* message of purpose and hope, we must carefully tailor our Scripture-engagement tools to define what the Bible says, what Christianity means, and how salvation is received and lived out in daily life. This has become our aim, and this is why our resources have proven so effective in transforming young lives by God's power, as you will see in Sonia's story.

SONIA

Sonia was a young Colombian girl who lived in Comuna 13, a neighborhood strictly under the control of an armed rebel group, and it had been for years. Sonia's family lived there, and her father worked there, but they knew the dangers. The police didn't come here to protect citizens. Sometimes soldiers came to engage the local rebel militia in a firefight, but otherwise this wasn't "Colombia." It was rebel territory.

This fact brutally intruded on the family one night when gunmen came to the house and demanded that Sonia's older brother join them. Her father and mother objected and told the thugs that their boy wasn't going to become a rebel, and the gunmen gave them two hours to rethink their answer. They'd be back then either to take the boy away to become a rebel fighter or kill everyone in the house.

With only one hundred twenty desperate minutes to prepare, the family packed up what they could and fled from their home, running for their very lives!

They went to Bogotá with nothing other than the possessions they could carry. But at least their son was safe from the armed rebel group. And thankfully another family offered to take them in. This was a godsend—or so it seemed. Now they had a place to stay while they tried to get their lives back in order. Young teenager Sonia was naturally upset by their narrow escape from the militia, but she too was glad to have a safe place to stay—until the man of the house raped her.

Sonia was shattered by the experience. And when it became apparent that the rape had left her pregnant, she was devastated. Her first thought was that she had to abort the baby and try to forget all about this horror. But a local church had also reached out to Sonia's family, and she had received her own copy of the *Book of Hope*. The pastoral care she received and the promises of God in the Scripture book convinced Sonia that God still loved her and her unborn baby.

Today she is walking with the Savior and wants to raise her son, Angel, to follow Jesus Christ. One reason that Sonia's *Book of Hope* was able to communicate the love of Christ and His healing touch to her is because of the research we've done that reveals the heartfelt needs of the next generation, so we can tailor Scripture-engagement tools to give them spiritual answers to their most important questions. Colombia was among the first nations in which this intensive research was completed, and the findings amazed even the local Christians and church leaders.

The people of Colombia have long prided themselves on the strength of their families. The research showed that 58 percent of young people say their parents are the biggest influence in their lives, but the research also showed that 44 percent of Colombian young people almost *never* speak to their fathers about personal matters and 21 percent wonder if their fathers even love them. Although 90 percent agreed that marriage is meant to last a lifetime, most also doubted whether they would have a long-lasting marriage. This disconnect was not so hard to understand in light of other seemingly contradictory findings such as the fact that 79 percent said the Bible provides absolute moral truths that are the same for all people in every situation, yet 78 percent said that truth can be defined in two contradictory ways and still be correct. Or the fact that 81 percent say that all "good" people go to heaven, while 66 percent say that anyone who has not accepted Christ is going to hell. Again we see young people clearly conflicted because they're attempting to believe two contradictory things at once.

While these findings indicated the attitudes and contradictory *beliefs* of Colombian youth, other findings painted a picture of their *behaviors*: 91 percent were drug-free—a great sign. But 30 percent had been legally drunk at least one time in the previous three months. Most said a high degree of integrity was important in their daily lives, but more than 70 percent had lied to an adult or friend in the past three months, and 70 percent thought it was fine to break the law if no one got hurt. The perilous moral terrain combined with the cognitive dissonance of living lives in conflict with the standards they want to maintain is taking a toll on Colombia's young people. Tragically the research further showed that nearly a quarter of Colombian children and youth have considered suicide.

These factors and many of our other research findings are

helping to shape new programs and Scripture-engagement tools that will connect with Colombian young people like Sonia to help them find the biblical message of purpose and hope as a foundation for a lifelong relationship with Jesus Christ.

Today many of the oldest OneHope programs—what we call our "legacy programs"—continue to function much as they did in the past. All new programs are developed and tested according to our new model, and about one-third of existing programs are being evaluated for fruitfulness on an ongoing basis. By the end of 2015 we expect to be evaluating *every* program with an eye toward increasing fruitfulness. In the next chapter I'll explain a little of how this evaluation is done.

I don't have the space to give you all the results of our research here, but you can find it online at www.spiritualstateofthechildren .com. If you're involved in ministry and want to use the research or explore ways OneHope can help you in engaging children and youth with God's Word, please check it out and contact us today. The United States is one of the countries where research has already been completed—and we'd love to help you affect destiny here at home or abroad.

And now, the big question...

WHAT HAPPENED IN SWAZILAND?

We never, that I know of, met up with the girl in the red sweater again. But our encounter with her helped us shape a new ministry model not only for her country but also globally. Our research showed us that many hundreds of thousands of young people in Swaziland were living in households led by children, far more than we'd realized. AIDS or the ancillary diseases and hardships having killed their parents and their extended families being too poor to provide for them, these little ones were trying to provide for themselves. Our new partners in that country took the research and ran with it. Together we created a program called In Community by Community, which helps churches adopt specific needy families.

This was a complete one-hundred-eighty-degree turn from the traditional school ministry we had at first attempted in Swaziland. This new outreach prequalifies the ones who will be delivering God's Word to the children as caring Christians, real believers who understand the gospel and desire to share it and see lives transformed. The program does not rely on the school system (or nominal Christians who may also be among the worst child predators in the nation). It's built instead on the commitment of believers who desire a unified outcome of transformed lives, of destiny affected.

Of course there are far more teachers and far better infrastructure for "distributing books" in the school system than there are dedicated believers willing to get involved in adopting a needy household. But the results, the *fruitfulness* of the new In Community by Community program, are much better. They are perhaps even life-saving in addition to being life-transforming, as local churches reach out to orphans and young people in child-led households with the love of God. We have no illusions that we've transformed a country overnight through the development of the program, but we do know that by God's grace, OneHope has made an authentic contribution to presenting the message of salvation and the opportunity for life-transformation to the next generation.

You have an authentic contribution to make too. You can be affecting destiny, if not for the next generation in Swaziland or Colombia, then for children in the underprivileged neighborhood across the highway or for the old folks in the nursing home down the street. I'm showing you how God is using some believers who are willing to obey, trust, and have faith in Him. How is He using you? Don't miss your chance to affect destiny.

Chapter 10

SEEN AND UNSEEN

I CAN SAY THAT today I am living in the unseen, miraculous power of God moment by moment. This life-transforming power is available not only to us but also to the children and youth of the world. The unseen, breaking into this visible "temporariness," lifts people up and gives them a hope and a future, an eternal but *unseen* hope and future, that invades our visible world. That's *affect destiny.*

Up to this point my life has taught me that the unseen miraculous can break into the everyday, visible world at any moment and dramatically rearrange things. I believe it because I've experienced it, and my life verse reflects it. What is unseen is eternal! And the eternal love of God is constantly reaching out to rescue, redeem, and embrace us. From my grandparents' miraculous conversion to my dad's extraordinary calling to be a seven-year-old preacher, to my own beautiful miracle of healing, the seen and unseen have become inseparable for me, because I know the unseen forces—the triumphs, challenges, and everything else in between—are always "achieving for us an eternal glory" (2 Cor. 4:17).

Yet in most of Africa the people have an entirely different idea about the unseen. They believe in the spirit world and the impact it has on every aspect of life. François's family, from the island nation of Madagascar, is a good example.

François

Friends and neighbors thought everything would be OK if François and his mother would just dig up the bones of their ancestors, clean them up, and try to appease their spirits. The widow and her son must have neglected the spirits—why else would François's father have died, leaving François and his mother alone with no means of support?

This was the folk wisdom of Madagascar, a nation where most people say they are Christians, but at the same time they pray to their ancestors, fear ghosts will follow them home from a funeral, and believe they shouldn't kick a wall because it will mean death for their grandmas. Somehow the spirit-worship of the island's ancient African forebears has survived and become syncretized with Christianity.

For François and his mother no amount of ancestor worship was going to help them survive. An uneducated single mom in their poor neighborhood had only limited choices to try to earn a living. She arose before daybreak every morning to scour the area for the cheapest vegetables she could find, then she walked many weary miles trying to sell them. Sometimes she made enough money to buy a little rice. Other times she came home with the dregs of the vegetables, and this was dinner for her and her son. Sometimes they just went without food altogether.

When François's uncle came to town and asked if François could come live with him to help him mine for gold, François was curious. He didn't want to leave his mother, but at the same time he knew he was a burden to her, and his uncle would at least feed him—or so he thought. In fact, his uncle took him away to another town and began using him as slave labor, in addition to abusing and starving him. François wasn't allowed to go to school, and for months he wore only the clothes on his back, the same ones he had arrived in. One time his mother called to ask how things were going, and François desperately wanted to tell her what his uncle was doing to him. But his uncle was right there beside him, and he was afraid to say anything.

Things were getting desperate. François stumbled upon his uncle's plans to *sell him* to another man—apparently he was worth more in cash than in the unpaid labor he was doing for his uncle. Now François was terrified. The next time his uncle sent him out on an errand, he begged enough money from strangers in the market to use a pay phone and contact his mother. He told her what had happened; she told him to come home right away. It was a narrow escape, but the boy managed to get away from his uncle and back to the town where his mother was.

It felt like a second chance, yet François and his mother still struggled to survive. François went back to school, but he was a charity case at the Catholic school. When the funding dried up, he had to quit. His mother couldn't pay the fees, and the school couldn't provide for him anymore. Things seemed as bleak as ever for François. He joined his mother on her vegetable route, trudging through the heat of the day with no food or water and knowing there was no rice at home.

The director of the Catholic school kept in touch with François and knew about his situation. Whenever he could, he hired François for odd jobs around the school. When our team came to talk to the school director about showing *The GodMan* and distributing the *Book of Hope,* the man gratefully accepted—and he thought about François. He wasn't a student, but he hoped François could still get a *Book of Hope.* The school director asked our church partners whether he could also invite nonstudents. (About half of Madagascar's children don't attend school.) Our team was delighted, and of course they said yes! "The Word of God is for everyone," they assured him.

So with many other unenrolled children François came to school for the showing of the film and to receive his own *Book of Hope.* By this time, of course, he already knew how to read. He loved the book and the film! They made Jesus so real to him! François knew his neighbors thought he and his mother should try to gain the favor of their ancestors or see a witch doctor to rid them of the evil curse they were under, but after his encounter with Jesus Christ, François knew that what he and his mother needed wasn't the intervention of dead ancestors but the love of the Savior! Today François is a committed follower of Christ, and he has also shared his faith with his mother. She too chose to follow Jesus!

Our church partners in their town launched a Bible club for children and youth that François began attending faithfully; he also began doing work around the church center that serves the poor and needy, as he had done for the Catholic school. Today nineteen-year-old François has been discipled and cared for by his church family. He and his mother still live in poverty, but with the money he makes working at the church, he contributes to their small income. He dreams of the day he can do even more. He wants for his mother to be able to retire from the vegetable business, and he would like to build a house for her.

His heart is passionate about sharing his faith. As much as he can, François travels with teams from his church, sharing *The GodMan* film and the *Book of Hope* with other Malagasy children and youth. François tells them from the heart how God's love gave him a second chance at life and how different everything is now from those dark days when he was hungry, abused, and hopeless. His witness is powerful, and he has helped share the Word of God with many other young people. His destiny was affected by the intervention of a loving Savior through the obedience of our amazing local partners and the obedience and generosity of someone who cared enough to give so that François and his family could have God's Word and be transformed.

At the center of François's story and the story of our OneHope efforts in Madagascar is the strange fusion of Christianity and ancestor worship that prevents so many millions from coming to know the truth of the gospel. But with statistics that show that most people in Madagascar consider themselves Christians—either

Catholic or Protestant—how could we know that the nation is still a massive mission field? It took digging into the true attitudes, beliefs, and behaviors of the young people to discover the extent of the problem and shaping programs that addressed it. This is the story of the Spiritual State of the World's Children research in Madagascar, and particularly how an encounter with God's Word manages to dramatically change the attitudes, beliefs, and behaviors of those who experience it.

THE *BOOK OF HOPE* INSPIRES LASTING CHANGE

The question was: Why did people who had churches and claimed to be Christians still adhere to ancient tribal religions and superstitions? The answer seemed to be that, although they *attended* churches and perhaps even took part in church *rituals*, they did not actually know what the Bible said or they did not understand what the Bible meant. The *Book of Hope* is designed to communicate clearly the gospel message through the story of the life of Christ. Could it also help children and youth develop basic Bible literacy that they had not grasped before?

Our team designed a survey to test the hypothesis. We surveyed the young people who were going to receive the *Book of Hope* about the problems that church leaders said plagued many "Christians" of Madagascar—ancestor worship, witchcraft, and superstition. Our team came up with a series of statements with which survey respondents could agree, disagree, or say that they were neutral (or hadn't made up their mind). Our plan was to administer the survey once before students received the *Book of Hope*, again a few weeks after they had read it, and then again several months later. This would give us a look at the immediate effects and then the longer-term effects of their experience with God's Word. I would love to roll out the entire project and results for you here, but let me try to condense it by showing you just a few key statistics.

- Pre–*Book of Hope*: 52 percent of Malagasy young people did not disagree that, "Sometimes you must dig up a dead family member to talk to them, so they can pray to God for you" (28 percent agreed, and 24 percent were neutral). After receiving the *Book of Hope*, only 23 percent agreed, while 28 percent were neutral, but months later, when resurveyed, fully 68 percent disagreed, and only 9 percent agreed.

- Pre–*Book of Hope*, 54 percent did not disagree with the statement, "If someone dies, the spirit of the dead person will have the same power as God" (25 percent agreed, and 29 percent were neutral). Months after receiving the *Book of Hope*, 65 percent disagreed, and only 8 percent agreed.

- Pre–*Book of Hope*, 53 percent did not disagree with the statement, "Ghosts are a part of my life" (28 percent agreed, and 25 percent were neutral). Months after receiving the Book of Hope, 65 percent disagreed and only 9 percent agreed.

- Pre–*Book of Hope*, fully 37 percent agreed that "the covering they put on a dead person is important to keep because it is very valuable and gives a special blessing" (27 percent were neutral). Just after the children and youth received the *Book of Hope*, agreement fell to 32 percent, and several months later, the number dropped to 20 percent, while 56 percent disagreed.

- Pre–*Book of Hope*, an astounding 45 percent agreed that "after a funeral, it is important to build a fire outside your home to keep the ghosts out." Only 34 percent disagreed. Just after receiving the book, agreement dropped to 37 percent, and months later only 21 percent agreed, while 53 percent disagreed.

As you can see from the survey results, meaningful interaction with the Word of God changes attitudes and beliefs in significant ways. Some of the other very heartening results of the survey showed that the *more* the child or youth engaged with God's Word, the greater the change in their attitudes and beliefs. For instance:

- Significantly more of those who have read most or all of the *Book of Hope* (59 percent) strongly disagree with the statement, "You must pray to both God and the ancestors at the same time," than those who have read only some of the book (47 percent).

- Significantly more of those who have read most or all of the *Book of Hope* (67 percent) strongly disagree with the statement, "If someone is sick, a witch-doctor can help them get better," than those who have read only some of the book (51 percent).

- When asked, "What other beliefs do you have besides, or alongside, believing in Jesus?" significantly more of those who have read most or all of the *Book of Hope* (74 percent) said, "None," as compared to 59 percent who had read only part of the book.

These changes in attitudes and beliefs don't take place in a vacuum of course. OneHope goes into nations where local believers are already addressing the heartfelt needs of the next generation. We work with church and ministry partners who want to present Christ to children and youth and help them find a new way of living in a relationship with Jesus Christ and who are looking for more effective tools to engage young people. François's story, for instance, highlights a local church program called Kelimahefa, a children's Bible club where young people meet every week to learn more about Jesus and how to follow Him. (This church also conducts special outreaches among the impoverished of the neighborhood, helping to meet physical needs as well as spiritual ones.)

While this outcome-based research project has focused on the results of interaction with the *Book of Hope,* you'll remember that about half of Madagascar's young people don't go to school and can't read. The Kelimahefa club and our other church partners also make extensive use of *The GodMan* film and our Storying Edition *Book of Hope,* containing illustrations from the film and very few words. It's a great combination for presenting the gospel to those who can't read. In fact, it was a plea from a missionary in Madagascar to have some tool to reach illiterate children that inspired us to create *The GodMan* film in the first place.

Joining hands with local churches and ministries is the most effective way to present the next generation with the gospel, and it's one of the primary foundations of OneHope. It's just the right way to do effective missions.

The research and surveys we've developed to create meaningful Scripture tools and test their effectiveness helped me to keep the covenant I made with God in Swaziland—a covenant to ensure we were creating the best possible resources to present the gospel to the next generation and to gauge their efficacy, so we could know that lives were truly being transformed.

CONTEXTUALIZING TOOLS FOR SHARING THE GOSPEL

Another important way we've improved Scripture-engagement tools like the *Book of Hope* and *The GodMan* film is through the process of contextualization, making sure the resources make sense in the context in which they're received. Consider these words from the apostle Paul in 1 Corinthians 9:19–23:

Though I am free and belong to no one, I make myself a slave to everyone, to win as many as possible. To the Jews I became like a Jew, to win the Jews. To those under the law I became like one under the law (though I myself am not under the law), so as to win those under the law. To those not having the law I became like one not having the law (though I am not free from God's law but am under Christ's law), so as to win those not having the law. To the weak I became weak, to win the weak. I have become all things to all men so that by all possible means I might save some. I do all this for the sake of the gospel, that I may share in its blessings.

His emphasis seemed to be, as ours is, on reducing barriers to the gospel. He would not "water down" the truth, but he would jettison nonessentials in order to make it as easy as possible for his audience to understand and respond. I remember during the contextualization process of *The GodMan* film for India, focus groups told us we should change the Nicodemus character's appearance because his bushy beard made him look like a Sikh (an individual marked by rejection of idolatry and caste), and of course we were portraying a Hebrew teacher of the law. It seems a small thing, but it's one less red flag put up against the gospel.

The GodMan film's animation portions are computer-generated graphics and generally fairly easy to contextualize to various cultures. The film also includes live-action "wraps," that is, a story of some young people from the particular culture, portraying their heartfelt needs and how the biblical message of purpose and hope meets those needs. The Indian film, for instance, portrays two Indian children running away from home on one of the ubiquitous Indian trains. It's a specifically Indian story in a specifically Indian setting that speaks to Indian children. In Africa the contextualized version of the film has a live-action introduction and conclusion that focus on three children on their way to a soccer game. As they're walking to the game, they're discussing their problems. One child has lost a parent. (Africa's AIDS epidemic makes this story all too common.) Another is the victim of abuse and neglect at home at the hands of a drunken father (also a common occurrence).

These stories help show how the gospel relates to the children in their culture, with their specific needs. It draws young people in and helps them see what Jesus *can* mean to them.

"Contextualization is simply an attempt to take off Western wrappings, which have typically become a part of worldwide Christianity, and put on 'clothing' that looks and feels much more natural and 'right' to the Hindu, Muslim, Buddhist, or anyone else," writes John Bailey in the Globe Serve Journal of Missions.[1] "The church owes to the peoples of the world an understandable hearing of the unchanging gospel."[2]

We actually see this process in the Bible itself. For example, the apostle Paul had a distinct style of presenting the good news to the Greeks at Mars Hill (Acts 17:22–34) that differed widely from the way he approached the topic with his fellow Jews (Acts 13:13–43). He knew the Greeks were polytheistic, an idea that was appalling to him. But he did not let his disdain for their ideas prevent him from sharing the gospel in the way he felt they would best understand. He took the time and trouble to think out a presentation that would appeal to them and help them understand the good news.

The Lord Jesus continually matched the stories He told to the audiences He was addressing. How many parables and teachings of Christ reference the seed and the sower, something everyone in ancient Palestine would have understood easily? When He spoke with the woman at the well, He began with something she would understand and be interested in—water. And of course the Holy Spirit Himself instituted the first contextualization of the gospel message on the Day of Pentecost, when He gave the gift of various languages to the one hundred twenty to testify of Him.

When we contextualize Scripture-engagement tools to target

various cultures, we're following a Spirit-inspired tradition that makes the Word of God accessible to all. We know it works, because we have our outcomes regularly tested. And it's right that we do so to do ministry smarter, more efficiently, more cost effectively, and with the greatest potential for transformed lives. But we also can't forget that this transformation comes "'not by might nor by power, but by my Spirit,' says the LORD of hosts" (Zech. 4:6, NKJV).

This idea of contextualization, though, is God's directive and not just for me, at the head of a global ministry—but for every believer. For you too. It's easy to see that OneHope has an obligation to contextualize the gospel for the fast-changing culture all around us. But you're part of the culture too, and your witness can also contextualize the good news for the people around *you*.

Without compromising the essentialities of the gospel, God is calling us to reach out to the children of our own neighborhoods and communities and affect their destiny. The United States is no longer a homogenous culture; it is diverse. If God has placed in your heart a desire to affect the destiny of your city, keep in mind that some of the most open, lonely, and spiritually hungry people have come here from other nations. They hold diverse worldviews and are waiting for someone like you to contextualize a loving message of hope so they can live a life of abundance that Jesus promises. They are waiting for you to open the door for them to hope for eternity.

How are you affecting their destiny today? If we can help you in any way, we want to.

Chapter 11

A BETTER MOUSETRAP

WE DO RESEARCH to understand the heartfelt needs of the next generation.

We design Scripture products tailored to speak to those needs.

We test the effectiveness of those tools and revise them for maximum impact.

We measure the outcomes of individual resources to judge their power to effect change.

But when you get right down to it, are we just building a better mousetrap? After all, the Bible says, "All Scripture is God-breathed and is useful for teaching" (2 Tim. 3:16).

Yes, God loves with an everlasting love, and He will have His way no matter what. I believe that. But at the same time why would we *not* want to obey His call and present His truth in the most effective way to the next generation? Why would we *not* pursue fruitfulness with all our God-given power and abilities? If our stated goal is to affect destiny, then I think we *must* keep building a better mousetrap because then, as Ralph Waldo Emerson said, the whole world will beat a path to our door.

I saw this in action when I heard Lydia Wonget, our partner in Cameroon, speak about a man who had traveled hundreds of miles by bus through rough and perilous terrain from his home in Central African Republic (CAR). He had come on behalf of CAR's children to find Lydia and call out to her, "Come over here and help us!"

My travels have taken me all over the world, across the continent of Africa many times, and I am good at geography, but I knew almost nothing about this most troubled of nations. As I heard Lydia speaking about this man's visit, the Holy Spirit spoke to me so clearly, saying, "Go to Central African Republic."

This incredibly impoverished nation has been referred to as a "garbage dump" for Africa's child soldiers. As rebel groups are vanquished and kicked out of their own countries, the remnants are able to regroup and take up residence in camps in CAR. Nicholas Kristof of the *New York Times* has called CAR "one of the neediest countries in the world."[1] It's a nation blighted by war, violence, poverty, and hopelessness. I knew only the love of God could ever make a difference.

I saw young boys toting guns, entire villages leveled by rebel soldiers, and schools and hospitals destroyed or shut down. Children fortunate enough to go to school may share one book for every eight students. Many thousands of children roam the streets, orphaned or abandoned. There's no infrastructure. The government has been powerless to make any lasting changes. Central African Republic is perennially on the list of the world's ten poorest nations,[2] and the "misery quotient" for life there is beyond anything you can imagine.

Looking around at this devastation, it's easy to think that our small efforts can never make a difference. But God has promised to give us the nations as an inheritance. He has directed us to affect destiny, and He wouldn't give us a command without giving us the means to keep it. He says, "Ask of me, and I will make the nations your inheritance, the ends of the earth your possession" (Ps. 2:8). The hopelessness and poverty of CAR are no match for the prayers of God's people and the power of His Word. I know this, because of my own experience, and my dad's. Any time the Holy Spirit has ever spoken a word to us and we've been faithful to go where He directs, we have seen God affect the destiny of nations.

I've told you just in this book about my (albeit reluctant) visit to Kemerovo in Russia, and my dad's trip to British Guyana when he was just a seventeen-year-old evangelist, and his commitment to go visit the Green family, even when there was no place for it in his busy schedule. I could fill another book with the stories of astounding answers to prayer. There was the day it stormed all over the city except in the clear, sunshiny circle where a Romanian team was praying for good weather for their HopeFest Celebration. There was the team that prayed for a poor little Indian teenager to be delivered from oppression by evil spirits that caused her to have screaming fits—and she was completely set free by the power of God. Today she and her whole family are following Jesus!

We believe in the power of prayer, and we know our efforts to affect destiny only succeed when they're covered in prayer. So I knew, even though I was shocked by the poverty and misery of Central African Republic, that God had intended my being there for the good of the nation. I knew our prayers and His power would affect destiny here. And it was here I met a smiling, jovial man named Earnest. He was my driver and translator. I had come to interface with the prime minister, minister of education, local pastors, and other leaders to see how we could best partner with them to bring the hope of Jesus Christ to the next generation. As I made my round of meetings and learned one heartbreaking fact after another about CAR, Earnest was always there beside me. I noticed that many Christians greeted him as Pastor Earnest, and finally it occurred to me to ask him, "What's your story? Are you a pastor?"

"I guess I am," he said.

And I guess he *was*. This was the story he told...

EARNEST

He'd been one of those abandoned street children. His father had abused and beaten him, and finally when Earnest was ten years old, he couldn't take it anymore. He ran away. He lived on the streets for years. He told me he couldn't remember ever going to sleep when he didn't feel hungry. Then a Muslim charity came in and began a feeding program. Earnest learned that all he had to do to get a meal was convert to Islam. He gladly did! (Although the percentages vary widely depending on the source, Muslims are increasing numerically on a modest level but are seeing massive growth in influence and visibility, especially in cities. This growth usually happens in a number of countries where oil-rich Islamic nations have built schools and hospitals or provide feeding programs like this one, which entice people to convert.[3])

Earnest remained a Muslim as he lived on the streets until he was sixteen years old. Then one day he met a man who asked if he was hungry and invited him to come to a restaurant with him.

"When the food came, I was so hungry. I just wanted to dive in!" Earnest told me. "But the man said, 'Wait, we have to pray.' He started to say grace, and he used the name 'Jesus.' I heard that name and something happened inside of my heart. I have no other way to describe it, but suddenly I felt such unbelievable love that right there I just began to weep."

Here was a tough boy who had raised himself on the streets suddenly overcome by the love of Jesus when he heard the name for the first time! His kindly benefactor told him all about the Savior, and right there Earnest committed his life to Christ. As he told me this story, his big smile broke out again, and I could almost feel the same wonder he had felt when Jesus reached out to embrace him on that day. He didn't read a Bible or see a movie. He just heard the name of the Savior, and the unseen world broke into his life and claimed him as Christ's own.

But the miraculous doesn't end there.

"I've served Jesus ever since," Earnest told me. But one thing bothered him. "When I turned seventeen, I had such a desire. The thing I wanted more than anything in life was to be able to read. I wanted that more than food. But I never learned how to read. I was completely illiterate. I would pray, 'Lord, I want to read Your Word so bad. Please teach me how to read.'" And God answered his prayer!

He was given the gift of literacy. And today he can read in English, Sango, the language of the indigenous of CAR, and the official French languages. Because he could read, by God's grace and miraculous power, he was able to start a small business, which became very successful. He and his wife have built a church in the back of their shop (which is also their home); there many of their neighbors now come together to worship.

"So I guess I am a pastor now," he said.

God did this creative miracle to transform Earnest's life, based on nothing but the willingness of one Christian man to buy a meal and share the gospel with a young man living on the street. This is "affect destiny"—for a man to take time to invite a street child out to lunch and the result is that everything in the boy's life, and so many others, is transformed forever. I wonder how many affect destiny moments like this I have missed in my life.

Our hope and prayer is that, as a ministry, OneHope never misses these moments! I pray, as a Christ-follower, you don't miss them either.

There are so many stories I could tell you to explain "affect destiny" to show you how God's Word transforms completely, especially when it places a child in a local faith community where he can grow in God. Let me share Miguel's story with you. But to fully understand it, you have to come with me to Brazil—to a *tenda de umbanda*. What is it? Take a look.

MIGUEL

Around the room small idols sit with offerings of anointed foods and wine in front of them. Drums are beating. The tinkling sound of the agogô bell keeps rhythmic time to the sounds of chanting, then singing. The crowd of initiates is dancing in time with the pounding of the music; the priestess, or "mother of saints," encourages the faithful to welcome the spirits into their bodies. Cigar smoke fills the air—it's thought to purify evil and invite the presence of the ancient African deities who are worshipped here. Then, as the drumming, chanting, and dancing reach fever pitch, a change comes over some of the dancers. Their bodies begin to contort, and their faces take on wild expressions.

The way they begin to move, to dance, walk, or shuffle, indicates what spirit has possessed them. A young man suddenly needs a cane to lean on, and with a straw hat on his head, he sits down with legs spread apart, back bent, elbows on knees, places a pipe in his mouth, and becomes the image of a *preto velho*—an "old black man," an African slave who died on a Brazilian plantation two hundred years ago. Those who seek his simple wisdom line up to consult him.

The old woman whose wrinkled face lights up with slavering lust as she begins to dance suggestively, grinding her hips and gesturing with her hands for others to come and join her, reflects a *pomba gira*. She is possessed by a spirit said to be beautiful and insatiable—the personification of female sexuality. Heterosexual and homosexual women seeking advice in matters of the heart surround the *pomba gira* and seek her counsel.

The chanting, singing, dancing, and drumming continue as other initiates become possessed. Then in the crowded audience simply *watching* this spiritist ritual, a noninitiate falls under the spell, possessed. She's whirling in an angry war dance, her feet pounding. The *mãe de santo* priestess rushes to her side, helping her into the crowd with the other initiates, who place a pearl crown on her head with a veil to hide her face. She is channeling Yansã, goddess of winds and storms, and the crown and veil are her regalia. Later, when the spirit leaves her, the woman will be invited to become an initiate, since she has already been so favored by the spirits.

This is the *tenda de umbanda*, a sort of singing, dancing, drumming séance that has been taking place for decades in Brazil, where

Afro-Brazilian cults such as *Umbanda, Candomble,* and *Macumba* are celebrated (and protected) as part of the nation's history—and a boon to the tourist industry.[4] Most *tendas* are open to the public and sometimes draw great crowds. The cults are said to be continuations of ancient African religions brought to Brazil by African slaves. As followers of Christ, we would consider them nothing more than witchcraft and demonism, for there's no denying that supernatural events take place and people *do* become possessed. Our ministry partners in Brazil say some of these demon possessions result in the human hosts engaging in sexual perversion, violence, and even animal sacrifice.

This was the environment in which a little boy named Miguel was growing up. His grandmother was one of their community's most popular and powerful *mãe de santo* mediums, and their home was a large *terreiro de umbanda,* basically a temple for the rituals. Everyone in the family—aunts, uncles, and cousins—was involved in the cult in some way. Even child initiates can be present for the ceremonies, learning to identify the possessing spirits and aiding them if possible. But for Miguel, it was frightening to see the adults in his family take on these strange spirit personalities, to see his own grandmother and mother disappear, and a demon speaking through them. Worse yet, he knew he would be expected to become a spirit medium as well when he grew up and let the ancient deities into his own body and mind.

"I lived sad," Miguel remembers, "with a feeling of emptiness, not knowing what to do or how the future would be."

In many parts of Brazil the observance of these Afro-Brazilian rites has formed a sort of shadow society in which poor Brazilians of African descent have created their own hierarchy and community,[5] so that a successful *terreiro* confers honor and some prosperity on the founding medium. Miguel's parents and their siblings were expected to continue in the cult and "take over the business" from Grandma some day. Eventually Miguel too would be drawn in.

But God had another path marked out for Miguel and his family. Their *terreiro* was adjacent to an evangelical church. *Umbanda* is a syncretism of African mysticism and Catholicism, with many Catholic saints doing double-duty as ancient African spirits and deities.[6] So Miguel's parents were familiar with some aspects of Christianity, and they began attending the evangelical church. They soon came to know Jesus Christ as Savior.

Miguel was impressed by the change in them. He thought they were like new people! They *felt* like new people—happier, more relaxed, and filled with joy. They wanted to share with their son what they'd found. But it was so different from anything anyone in their family had ever experienced before, they weren't sure how to do it.

And then there was the problem with the government. Brazilian law protects the African rites as the nation's cultural heritage, and in many ways restricts people of other religions from sharing their faith with practitioners of Umbanda, Candomblé, Macumba, and other Afro-Brazilian cults.

Thankfully the church had a plan. *The GodMan* film is a great form of entertainment for children, *and* it clearly shows the life of Christ and the meaning of salvation. It's a nonaggressive way to present the truth of the Savior to boys and girls and help them see how following Jesus brings them hope for today and for eternity. When Miguel saw the film, he first began to understand what had happened to his parents to change them and bring them such joy.

"I was truly impressed, mainly with the crucifixion and resurrection of Jesus," he says. "After I watched the film, I decided to give my life to Jesus. Now I have joy, I'm content, and even in school I'm doing better."

Miguel and his parents experienced such dramatic life transformation that other members of the family began going to church just to see what it was all about. A few months after Miguel chose to follow Jesus, he and eighteen members of his family were baptized!

They have all chosen to leave the cult and are attending church together, seeking only the power of the Holy Spirit in their lives.

"With my family following Jesus, the relationship in our home is better," Miguel says. "I thank God for the people He used to teach my family about Jesus. My uncles, aunts, cousins, and nieces follow this way now. I just miss my grandmother; she didn't come yet."

Miguel's grandma is still conducting *terreiro de umbanda* rituals in her home. But with her whole family serving God and praying for her, I wonder how long it will be before she too makes the decision to come to Christ!

I love hearing stories like this, and because of my position as president of OneHope I hear a lot of them. They show me that when we are careful to create Scripture resources that engage young people with the answers to their most heartfelt needs, by God's grace, we're on the right track, and we're making a difference! You may call it building a better mousetrap or dressing the gospel up in a prettier costume, but just consider what this accomplishes.

It affects destiny, in this life and forever.

Chapter 12

WAKE UP AND FIGHT

NOW YOU KNOW what I do. Just as I told you in the beginning of this book, I fight for the next generation's right to receive the biblical message of purpose and hope that can transform their lives today, tomorrow, and for eternity. To me it's the most important work in the world. I hope you're also engaged in this battle. And I'd like to introduce you to another fighter. I've changed her name to tell you this story. I was listening to one of the most passionate ministry presentations I had ever heard by a young Latina ministry leader. Seldom have I heard someone so young present in such a confident way. Little did I know that I had played a part in her destiny. She was the eldest of three children, and her father had abandoned the family.

As a baby Theresa had been very sick. Her mother was poor but dedicated to her children and determined to do whatever she could to make sure Theresa was cured and grew up healthy. She left behind her native Puerto Rico and came to the United States, where she knew her child would get proper medical treatment.

Theresa's mother was strong, both in her will and in her body. Her determination and strength were an inspiration to young Theresa. Despite their poverty the family was hanging together in Miami, until a few years later when Theresa's mother met someone and fell in love.

"This was literally the beginning of the end for us," Theresa says.

Her mother moved the new boyfriend into their apartment, and he quickly showed his true colors: he was an alcoholic and drug addict and began to abuse Theresa's mother.

Night after night Theresa marshaled her little brother and sister to bed as they heard shouting and blows in the next room. Theresa tried to be strong and assure the little ones everything would be OK. She'd sing a lullaby to drown out the awful noise. She'd try to help her little brother and sister go to sleep, while she remained awake and vigilant, terrified and heartbroken.

Then one night Theresa heard the most unexpected sound. Her mother—her strong, capable mother—was whimpering in pain where she lay on her bed. The boyfriend had beaten her so thoroughly that all she could do was cry in pain. This thought horrified Theresa, but what she heard next was even worse.

"If you dare get up off that bed, I'll kill those children!"

Theresa peeped out the bedroom door. She saw the man getting a big butcher knife from the kitchen. Then he was coming right toward their room! She scurried back to bed with the others. In seconds the door opened. There stood their mother's boyfriend, his hands behind his back. "It's all right, guys. Don't worry," he told them. But Theresa knew he held a deadly weapon.

In that moment she began to see that perhaps her mother stayed with this man and allowed him to abuse her because she was afraid he would kill her children if she didn't. That night, thank God, the violence didn't escalate any further. Theresa decided that next time she and her siblings would flee, and then her mother would know they were safe and she would be able to fight back. But their escape never happened. Theresa was too young to know that sometimes adults stay in abusive situations for reasons that no one can fathom.

The abuse, the fighting, and the terror went on for years. Theresa grew into a beautiful teenage girl, and her mother's boyfriend began sexually abusing *her*. Rage battled with fear. Theresa longed to tell her mother what had happened. But at the same time she knew her mother already labored under so much anxiety and so much stress that the daughter was loath to add more troubles to her mother's already troubled world. So Theresa never said a word. Soon the man was sexually abusing Theresa every time her mother's back was turned and every time they were in the apartment and her mother wasn't there. The shame and grief were devastating to Theresa, but the thought of what it would do to her mother, if she knew, kept her silent.

Years went by. "I didn't tell my mother," Theresa remembers, "because I said, 'That's the sacrifice that I'm going to give my mom. I don't need to bring additional stress, additional strife, additional anxiety to her, so I'm going to keep that to myself. That's my gift to my mother. In just a couple years I'm going to go to college, and this will be over. I'm going to keep it a secret.'"

While a victim of sexual abuse can refuse to reveal the sad truth, the impact of it, the effect on the mind and spirit, can't be completely repressed. It was like a huge weight on Theresa's shoulders—every day, every moment—and slowly the anger and grief were working their way out. Finally, after yet another horrifying incidence of abuse, she blew up and told her mother what had happened—what had been going on for years! Amazingly Theresa saw a flash of the mother she used to know, the strong woman who had given up everything to come to the United States and make sure her baby got the best medical care. She rallied and kicked her boyfriend out of their home for good.

"I said, 'Praise God! Now everything is going to be all right!'" Theresa says.

But it wasn't all right. Yes, they were free from the fear and the abuse, but Theresa watched her mother deflate and fall into deep depression. She withdrew from the children and everything, except her struggle to provide for them. She was much less alive and happy now that they were free than she had been when she was enslaved to her abusive boyfriend. Theresa's momentary reaction of "Praise God" turned into a bitter lament of "Why, God?"

They were Catholic, and Theresa had gotten the impression that God rewards good behavior and punishes bad behavior, so she had always tried to be a good girl. She was a straight-A student and had always been very obedient to her elders. It had accomplished nothing. She'd still been victimized and terrorized. Through the years she had begun to nurture resentment against a God who promised so much in return for good behavior and had given her so little reward—in fact, He had let her be punished again and again by sexual abuse.

"What kind of God is this who has forgotten me and my family?" she asked herself. If there were in fact a God, she didn't like Him and wasn't going to believe in Him. What had He ever done for her?

Her mother, although lost in her own depression, recognized that Theresa was going down a bad path and needed spiritual and emotional help. She made arrangements for her daughter to go on a retreat sponsored by their church. Theresa went because she was always a good girl, always obedient to her mother, but she went prepared with a laundry list of doubts about God, doubts about the theology of the Catholic Church, and anger at the way God had treated her and her family.

Once she arrived, though, things looked different to Theresa. For the first time in a long time she felt peaceful there. And for the first time ever in her life, she felt that she was in the presence of God. She actually heard His voice saying to her, "My child, trust Me. Trust Me. I have great things for you, but you need to trust Me."

When she returned from the retreat, she was wondering what great things there could be for her. She had returned to the exact same reality she had left. Her mother was still deep in depression. They were still struggling to survive, sometimes wondering where their next meal would come from. Maybe she *hadn't* heard God's voice after all. Maybe she had just been swept up in the emotion of the moment. Theresa began to doubt the promise she had heard.

Then a friend in her chemistry class at school gave her the *Book of Hope* and told her she would enjoy it. Theresa didn't know what it was, but she trusted her friend. She looked at the back cover of the book; it started out with these words: "It's never good enough. The future is so depressing. What's the point?"

"Oh my goodness!" Theresa exclaimed. "This is me! It's telling *my* life."

Now she was keenly interested to see what was inside, and at home that night she began to read. She had never owned a Bible. Her mother had a children's Scripture book in Spanish that she'd read to Theresa and her siblings when they were small, but Spanish was never the language of Theresa's heart. She understood very little about Jesus Christ, His life and teachings. But the *Book of Hope* offered more than the life of Christ story, as important as that is. It was filled with extra sections that spoke to the heartfelt needs of young people in the United States. That night Theresa found a section that began, "I can't stand my stepdad. I guess he doesn't care. I get so lonely." Again, Theresa recognized herself. The section went on to direct her back into the Scriptures.

"I read the verse from John 14 that says, 'Trust in God. Trust also in Me,'" Theresa recalls. "And Jesus goes on to say, 'I will come back and take you to be with Me.' And I thought to myself, 'Wow, He's going to come back for me. He's going to rescue me from this. And He really cares.'"

This book and this encounter with Jesus Christ in the pages of the book were the fulfillment of the promise God had made to her at the retreat. He had great things for her, and now they were beginning to happen!

Theresa chose to walk with Jesus Christ, and from that moment she was on fire with enthusiasm for Him. She found deep healing for the scars of her past. She plunged into her church, where she became part of the youth leadership, and soon heard a calling to freely give what she had received from the Lord.

What she had *planned* for her future was college, law school, and a career as an attorney, so she could make a lot of money and be able to take care of her mom and family. She had the grades to do it. But then, the summer she graduated with her bachelor's degree, she had an opportunity to serve through an internship in her old neighborhood, helping at-risk children and youth. She thought this would be "giving back" to the community. She didn't know it would change the course of her life. When the internship ended, she didn't leave the youth center. She stayed on for four years and then became the director.

One day a brokenhearted teenager told her a tragic story of abuse at the hands of her mother's boyfriend. Her mother had passed away, and she was being raised by a grandma, but she just didn't know what to do with the pain. It was destroying her life.

"That's when I found my purpose and my calling," Theresa says, "because I was able to look at her and say, 'There is a God who loves you, who's going to be there, who wants to heal you from this brokenness. He healed me, and He helped me.'"

Looking back on how God introduced Himself to her and began her healing in the pages of a Scripture book, Theresa realized this was how she could touch the lives of other young people in the United States who are broken, victimized, and struggling just to keep their heads up. Today she works at a major ministry.

"I oversee the dealings with the least, the last, and the lost," she says. "And I fight like you would not believe to remind people there are places in the United States where young people are being victimized, abused, and forgotten—because you may hear stories from India from the Middle East. You see the hurt and brokenness abroad, but maybe you forget there is that very same brokenness right here in our backyard. There are dark places in the United States where young people are forgotten. Young people are abandoned, and young people are outright victimized."

Theresa and her husband are also the leaders of their church youth ministry, and although it is painful for her to share the story of her past, she does so when it will help another young person find hope in Jesus Christ. She graciously allowed me to share it here (although she asked me to change some details, for the sake of her family), because she believes so strongly in the ministry of OneHope.

"We need to understand that for every statistic, there is a young person who has a face, who has a story, who has a name," she told me. "And I know, because I was destined to be one of those statistics until OneHope and your ministry came and saved my life."

Chills ran down my spine as I heard Theresa's story. What might her life have become had she not found the hope of Jesus Christ? She says it *saved her life.* Now you can see why one of my great passions is to *awaken the global church to the reality of what is happening with children and youth today.*

DON'T BREAK THE MIRROR

The research we've done has shocked church leaders in various nations. I still remember the day we revealed the results of our Spiritual State of the World's Children research for Malawi. The church leaders who had gathered to hear the results were *stunned.*

Malawi has had Christianity for one hundred fifty years. We can trace the church in this country back to the arrival of David Livingstone. Yet when Malawi's boys and girls answered questions about their faith, behaviors, family, and relationships, the answers were, quite frankly, uninformed, incorrect, and contradictory. If you had asked any pastor in Malawi about the issue of homosexuality, for instance, they would have said it is not even an issue; everyone in Malawi understands that homosexual acts are sinful. Yet the research showed that 30 percent of Malawi's young people approve same-sex marriage. The nation's Christian leaders never saw this coming. We learned:

- Fifty-three percent of the children pray and 36 percent read religious Scriptures daily, yet 85 percent do not believe that prayer can be practically effective.

- Ninety-two percent believe a close relationship with God is important to their future, yet 90 percent are not sure or do not believe God exists.

- Sixty percent are very close to their mothers, and 46 percent are very close to their fathers, yet 43 percent frequently wonder if their mothers love them and 37 percent wonder if their fathers love them.

- Seventy-five percent indicated that premarital sex for a couple in love is never acceptable, and 70 percent would like to be a virgin when they marry, but at the same time 24 percent of the respondents (including 29 percent of the older students and 36 percent of the males) have had sexual intercourse.

Of all the results of all of our research around the world this sort of information in Africa and elsewhere is perhaps the most troubling. It confirms a nominal Christianity, a syncretistic evangelicalism that is *growing* in global Christianity. It must be arrested, and the only way is to teach our children the whole truth of God's Word.

The results of the Malawi research were revealed in a meeting of denominational pastors and church leaders. None of them had dreamed that Malawi's children were so out of touch with the foundations of the faith. As the spiritual leaders of the nation, could they help but be shocked by the fact that the children apparently believed in so many mutually exclusive premises? But I remember their response, because my friend Rev. Lazarus Chakwera gave me a metaphor for how they felt. He said:

In my country we have a story about a man lost in the African jungle with no real idea even which way is north or south, east or west. He goes around in circles for days, the foliage so thick he doesn't even know which way the sun is coming up until it has appeared over the treetops.

As he thrashes blindly on, he finds on the ground a little looking glass, a mirror, and he holds it up to look into it. His beard is outgrown. His face is haggard. His eyes bloodshot. Disgusted by what he sees, he flings the mirror on the ground and stomps on it. But the mirror wasn't the problem. The problem was the man the mirror reflected.

When the pastors and church leaders of Malawi examined the results of the research on our next generation, we were looking into the mirror, and we didn't like what we saw. We were distressed by the ugliness we saw in the mirror, but determined to fix the problem rather than breaking the mirror.

They had to choose to look into the mirror and decide if they would believe that reality and do what they could to change it. Because the church has had such a long history in Malawi, its infrastructure is sound. It also has a great partner in Scripture Union, a venerable ministry to African children in the schools of many nations. One of the main problems had been relevant Scripture resources to help Malawi's children develop Bible literacy and moral foundations. I knew OneHope could supply these resources.

"I believe as we continue using the *Book of Hope, The GodMan* film, and other Scripture-engagement tools that target the important biblical messages that our young people desperately need, we can change the direction and destiny of our nation by transforming the beliefs, attitudes, and actions of our children," Rev. Chakwera has said.

I agree, and I am glad to be able to serve great Christian leaders like those of Malawi and around the world. This is where I see myself, and Theresa, and others who fight for the future of the next generation. We must awaken the church to the actual state of the world's children. And then we must do something about it. Together, hand in hand, we must affect their destinies one child at a time.

Chapter 13

SPIRITUAL JUSTICE

WHEN HE GOT shot, no one removed the bullet.

When he fell behind in the march, they beat him.

If he couldn't keep up, he knew he'd be left for dead.

Dennis had been kidnapped as a small boy and forced to become a child soldier. The LRA rebels in Northern Uganda had tortured and abused him, forced him to commit horrible atrocities and endure them himself. When his company came under fire by government forces, his arm was wounded and his commander killed. Another rebel commander "rescued" Dennis and installed him as a bodyguard.

Finally after more than two years in this hellish existence, Dennis seized his chance to escape. He found his way to the World Vision Center; it was here that he received medical attention, had the bullet removed from his arm, and was reunited with his family.

Yet the memories haunted him. The anger paralyzed him. Through the loving compassion of the believers who support World Vision, Dennis's body was healed, and he was restored to his family, but how could he go back after what he'd been through? He was filled with rage and feared his own memories. Compassion wasn't enough to bring peace to Dennis.

When he heard about God at his school, Dennis refused to listen and always tuned it out. Bitterness consumed him—until he received the *Book of Hope*. He listened closely to the OneHope team and read about the love of Jesus in his book. It was as if the clouds above him began to part. Finally the light of hope began to shine in! Dennis chose to follow Christ as his Savior. His church family came around him to show him more about walking with Christ, how to pray, and how to receive deep spiritual healing from the great physician. Slowly the anger began to seep away as the love of Christ began to fill Dennis's heart.

"It's no longer important for me to keep thinking on those other things that happened to me in the bush," Dennis says today. "I have forgiven those people. Now I have received Christ, and I know that God has forgiven me."

My daughters, Diandra and Natasha, belong to a generation of Western believers who have a great heart for binding up the wounds of broken children like Dennis, to feed the hungry and provide shelter for the homeless and clothing for the naked. They read Jesus's parable in Matthew 25, and they understand instinctively that to love as Christ loves is to pour out compassion on people in desperate need. But somehow the idea has slipped into the church in the United States that those works are "humanitarian," while the proclamation of the gospel is "evangelistic." Evangelism and compassion have been sundered, even pitted against each other, in a way that has caused our Christian young people to draw back in disgust at those whom they perceive would share the message of salvation but don't give a cup of cold water in Jesus's name. They want *social justice*, and I agree with them. But I think we, in the Western church, must also come back to the realization that social justice can never be until there is *spiritual justice*. Our Christian young people are zealous to feed, clothe, and heal. I am burdened to show them that it's the gospel that makes it possible for compassionate outreach to even bear lasting fruit.

I believe the church in the West must be called back to the truth that compassion *and* proclamation are both *evangelism*. There's no justice without Jesus.

TIFFANY

I think of Tiffany in Peru and the day her roof was repossessed. An armed rebel war had been waged across Peru's mountainous frontiers, and hundreds of thousands of peasants, *campesinos,* had been forced to flee their rural homes, seeking both refuge and employment in the big cities. Such were Tiffany's parents. They found no work and no hope in Lima. They joined thousands of squatters flinging up makeshift shacks in a "community" that came to be called San Juan de Lurigancho and came to be known for its poverty and hopelessness. Tiffany's parents built their new "home" with what they could scavenge. They had to buy the roof on credit. Every week they paid the contractor for the tin shingles that kept the rain out of their house.

This was the life Tiffany was born into. Her father, an artist, was forced to spend hours in backbreaking labor, picking up sticks, tin cans, discarded brick, and stone to try to sell to other refugees. It was the only way he could find to bring any money into the home, but it took its toll on his moody temperament. He started drinking to ease the pain of his sore muscles and the even more devastating pain in his heart and mind. His children were hungry. His wife had to work as a maid just to put food on the table. He had brought his family here, and now he had failed to provide for them. *He was a failure.* The oblivion of alcohol at least made him feel numb if he drank enough. If not he just became agitated and angry. He started slapping his wife and children around. Little Tiffany learned to fear those moods. And she would try to avoid her father if she could, but of course that was difficult in their tiny home.

Tiffany's mother worked hard to keep the family together, and Tiffany's older sister was soon put to work as a maid too. They pinned all their hopes on her older brother, who was now eligible to go to technical school. If they could all scrimp and save enough to get him through school, perhaps he could get a job with real skills and a regular paycheck! But the costs were so high for their meager means, and then there were other expenses. Mom wanted to keep little Tiffany in school too, and there were uniforms and supplies to purchase. And they had to eat. She rapidly fell behind in the bills. She missed several payments to the man who held the note on the roof they'd purchased on credit.

The day the workmen came to repossess the roof, our OneHope team was at nine-year-old Tiffany's school with the *Book of Hope* for the children. I remember the school itself was a wonderful standout in this poverty-stricken neighborhood. The dusty streets around it, lined with semi-permanent shacks—some of which had no running water—led to the wall around a spacious school with tidy buildings and classrooms, a very dedicated headmistress, and good-looking children who were dressed smartly in their uniforms. Once on the school grounds it was easy for us to forget the hunger and desperate need just outside. But we knew the children could never forget it; they lived it daily.

But Tiffany immediately captured our attention because she was so friendly and outgoing. Despite her difficult life of being reared in the hopelessness of San Juan de Lurigancho, with an abusive father and a mother who was barely hanging on, she was as bright as a lovely sunbeam. Like her father, she was already an artist and showed us several of her drawings. She was excited about receiving the *Book of Hope,* and she even invited the team to come home with her after school and meet her mama.

We were delighted! As we walked with Tiffany to her home, she chatted amiably with us about school, homework, her brother and sisters—their ages, what they did, and the place where her parents had come from. When we arrived at the house, we saw the work in progress. The contractor's men were dismantling the roof. It was clear Tiffany's mom wanted to be hospitable and invite us in, but how could she explain what was happening? It was a terrible moment for her, but of course Tiffany hadn't known it was happening and didn't quite understand it. After a short visit we invited Tiffany and her mother to the special outreaches taking place in San Juan de Lurigancho all that week. Then we left embarrassed, a little shaken, and wondering what we could do.

Our team was made up of a few volunteers from the United States and a few members of the local church. The fact is, we Americans probably could have pooled our cash and come up with the US dollars to pay for the roof. If we'd known in advance exactly what was happening, we might have thought to do it. But then what would have changed? Yes, the family would still have had a roof over their heads, and they would also still have had too many expenses, not enough income, and a papa who drank up whatever money he happened to make. As it turned out, what we had given Tiffany in the form of the gospel message was a far greater gift than any money or resources we could have donated.

Tiffany and her mom read through the *Book of Hope* that night. The next night they came to the HopeFest Celebration, and both dedicated their lives to Christ. Soon Tiffany's older sister and brother also chose to follow Jesus. Their neighborhood church surrounded them with love and support. Tiffany's dad, astounded by the transformation of his family, soon began attending church with them. Not too much later he stopped drinking and committed his life to Christ. The abuse stopped, and healing began. Once he had come out of the alcoholic haze, he was able to get steady work. Soon he moved the family out of San Juan de Lurigancho and into a middle-class neighborhood—into a home with a roof.

It was 1998 when Tiffany received the *Book of Hope* at school. Today at twenty-three years old she has completed a degree in pharmaceutical technology and pre-K education. She launched a preschool, called *Estrellitas de Amor*, or "Little Stars of Love." She still has her sweet smile and a spirit of infectious joy, which you can see shining through especially when she's working with her students. She employs two other teachers who help her with the student population of thirty-six little ones, ages three to five. She is also beginning a partnership with her local church and children's ministry. And she wants to continue her studies so she can expand her school and offer more grade levels to make Little Stars of Love a ministry for children whose families have few resources. Her papa, who once used to terrorize his family in drunken rages, is now the man Tiffany calls her "right hand" at her school. He works as a handyman and teacher's aide, and you can see the real joy of a redeemed life shining in his and Tiffany's eyes. What a transformation!

By God's grace we affected destiny for Tiffany—and her whole family—not with food and money, but with a biblical message of purpose and hope that put them on a path that led to amazing transformation for this life and an eternity with Christ. A roof alone couldn't have done that.

It's Not an Either-Or Proposition

This is why I say unless it is built upon spiritual justice, the working of social justice will always only be temporary. Even if it brings physical and material hope in this life, it cannot carry over into eternity. John Piper reminded me of this while I was attending the Lausanne Consultation on World Evangelism:

> If God had not put Christ forward to bear his own wrath, if Christ had not become a curse for us, as Galatians 3:13 says, then all the nations and all Jews would have perished under God's wrath and entered into everlasting suffering in hell, as Jesus said in Matthew 25:46. The reason I draw out this implication of the cross is to hold together in this congress and in the church of Christ two truths that are often felt to be at odds with each other, but don't have to be.
>
> One truth is that when the gospel takes root in our souls it impels us out toward the alleviation of all unjust suffering in this age. That's what love does! The other truth is that when the gospel takes root in our souls it awakens

us to the horrible reality of eternal suffering in hell, under the wrath of a just and omnipotent God. And it impels us to rescue the perishing and to warn people to flee from the wrath to come (1 Thessalonians 1:10).

I plead with you. Don't choose between those two truths. Embrace them both. It doesn't mean we all spend our time in the same way. God forbid. But it means we let the Bible define reality and define love.

Could Lausanne say—could the Evangelical church say— we Christians care about all suffering, especially eternal suffering? I hope we can say that. But if we feel resistant to saying "especially eternal suffering," or if we feel resistant to saying "we care about all suffering in this age," then either we have a defective view of hell or a defective heart. [1]

"Either we have a defective view of hell or a defective heart." What we want is the biblical view of hell and the heart of Jesus Christ. This, I think, is true social justice and true compassion both to alleviate suffering in this world and to connect people to the One whose sacrifice made a way for them to be spared eternal suffering. This is why missionaries of old went into the world and built not just churches but also hospitals, schools, and orphanages. Their definition of evangelism included the proclamation of the gospel and loving acts of charity and fellowship. It's like my friend Chris Hodges, pastor of Church of the Highlands in Birmingham, Alabama, declares, "Social justice without Jesus is no justice at all."

This ought to be our definition of evangelism today as well. Where we have let compassion vs. evangelism become an either/or proposition, we have failed in both.

This explains why right now I'm raising money for basketballs for Central African Republic.

I told you about the poverty there and the hopelessness, violence, and disease that blight this nation. We're doing what we can to change that. The minister of education has approved our Scripture resources to be incorporated into literacy programs in the schools. And in partnership with Hope Education Foundation, a non-governmental organization (NGO) with a strong track record of work with the Centers for Disease Control and Prevention (CDC) and US Agency for International Development (USAID), we are embarking on a deworming program for children who are vulnerable to parasites.

And then there is the basketball exchange program.

CAR has a passion for basketball. As I met with the minister of sports for the nation, I heard an interesting tale. In the 1960s and 1970s the Grace Brethren Fellowship in the United States sent short-term mission teams to CAR, and many of the team members were young people who played basketball. The then-king of Central African Republic fell in love with the sport. Once he started playing, everyone started playing. The majority of Sango people are tall, and they became very good basketball players. The CAR national team won the African Championship twice!

When the civil wars began, though, the land was devastated, and of course the basketball program was decimated too. But now the government has extended an invitation for us to organize Western coaches and players to come to CAR and help train their national team. The team would travel the country playing exhibition games for children, and *our* team would conduct skill drills and basketball camps and share the Word of God. We'd have governmental permission to teach young people (in schools and out) about determination, physical fitness, teamwork, character, integrity, and sportsmanship—and to introduce them to the Savior from whose mind all these concepts first flowed.

In CAR basketball equals evangelism. This is how it ought to work!

This is how it *did* work in South Africa and dozens of nations across Africa and Latin America in 2010. Only it was *futbol*, the game Americans call soccer. Leading up to the 2010 FIFA World Cup in South Africa, hundreds of churches and missions organizations conducted *futbol* camps and promoted soccer-themed rallies and events. Boys and girls who were *futbol*-crazy had the chance to practice new skills, play in competitions, receive a soccer ball of their own—and a Champions Edition *Book of Hope*, which introduced them to the life of Christ and the testimonies of many Christian professional soccer players.

Thousands of young people attended the camps and events, and many young lives were changed forever.

In Africa and Latin America soccer equals evangelism.

The gospel touches every area of our lives. The love of Christ transforms every area of our lives. It makes sense, then, that "evangelism" should embrace more than simply the proclamation of the good news and instead touch *every* area of our lives. Remember, when Jesus first announced His ministry of redemption, He quoted a passage from Isaiah. As recorded by Luke, He said:

> The Spirit of the Lord is upon Me, because He has anointed Me to preach the gospel to the poor; He has sent Me to heal the brokenhearted, to proclaim liberty to the captives and recovery of sight to the blind, to set at liberty those who are oppressed; to proclaim the acceptable year of the LORD.
>
> —LUKE 4:17–19, NKJV

Preaching is at the top of the list, but the tasks that follow it are ones of healing and liberation. These should be our priorities as well. And it's my contention that healing, liberation, feeding, and clothing are all, in fact, intended to be part of our preaching. Just as faith without works is dead, preaching without practical action is also dead.

This is, I think, a concept that must be reiterated in the Western church particularly. What I've seen of the *global* church (as opposed to the North American church) shows me that *they* already get it. In the poor areas of the world, churches that are growing and proclaiming the truth of God have already become the conveyors of social justice. They're already feeding the hungry and taking in the homeless. It is part and parcel of their proclamation of the good news to live the good news daily. In the United States we must follow their example. We must not divorce social justice from evangelism, and we must not divorce evangelism from social justice. Social betterment is not the mission of the church; it is the transformational fruit of a redeemed people living like Jesus.

When I say it's "our job," I don't just mean the job of the OneHope team and me. I mean the job of every follower of Christ who wants to build His kingdom. I mean it's my job, and *your* job too. When you stand to affect destiny, follow God's call to your own biblical ministry where you live, among the people you see every day, and reach out with His love and compassion, you are affecting destiny. You are bringing about the spiritual justice for which all creation groans. If you haven't yet discovered your position of power in Jesus Christ—your calling and your own destiny that will help shape destiny for others in need—I encourage you to seek God today. Discover the one important way, or the many and various ways, you can promote spiritual justice and affect destiny.

I was, as you might say, born into this calling. Maybe you were too. But maybe you weren't. Maybe you were somebody who *needed* spiritual justice, someone who benefited from another believer believing in you. Whatever the case you now know the love of Jesus, and knowing it, you want to share it. And you can! People in need aren't restricted to only being within Central African Republic or India. There are needy people in your own community or on the outskirts of it. When you become Christ to them, you're affecting their destiny and bringing about the spiritual justice that will one day rule in God's kingdom on earth. Don't delay. Don't wait and wonder whether this ministry is right for you. Roll up your sleeves and get to work. Deliver spiritual justice and affect destinies. It's your calling. It's my calling. It's our job!

Chapter 14

AND JUSTICE FOR ALL

I T'S EASY TO see that a kidnapped boy who has been forced to become a soldier deserves spiritual justice. It's easy to see that an impoverished child with no roof over her head deserves spiritual justice. Thinking back on Theresa, in chapter 12, it's easy to see that a teenager who has been sexually abused and left traumatized and hopeless deserves spiritual justice.

But there are huge segments of the global youth population who live in developed nations and have access to every luxury but are still denied spiritual justice because they've never received the gospel in a way they can understand and relate to. I'm thinking specifically about Japan. The nation of Japan had been on my heart for months before the tragic 2011 earthquake-tsunami-nuclear disaster. Part of my frustration in sharing the good news there is that the region was so completely resistant to the gospel. In Russia we might have a goal of touching the lives of four million young people with God's Word in a year, and in India, a goal of twenty million. But in Japan our goal is only maybe forty thousand. The schools weren't open to us. The majority of the population resolutely ignored Christian spirituality. Materialism had replaced even Buddhism and Shintoism as a daily reality for the people.

There was very little opportunity for discussing spiritual things with young people. They were too busy. The pressure is intense in

Japan for young people to succeed in school and commence making money.

And many Western churches and missions organizations seemed indifferent. Although Japan's economy had been rocked by the global recession, it was still seen as a wealthy, industrial first world nation. What need for compassionate aid was there? Who could get interested in helping children and youth who had enough to eat, nice clothes, and all the latest gadgets? Again, here is this false dichotomy between the physical and the spiritual, between compassion and evangelism. Did the fact that Japanese children had enough to eat mean that they had no problems or that they were going to heaven? Of course not!

The problems of Japan's next generation are severe.

Thousands of Japanese boys and young men (even some young women) have become *hikikomori*, meaning withdrawn or pulling away. It is used as a noun or an adjective like "alcoholic." *Hikikomori* shut themselves into their bedrooms one day and don't come out again. If they stay in for six months, they're officially considered *hikikomori*—some stay in for years. The pressure of school, the threats of bullies, and the fear of the future are all too much for them, and they would rather be in their bedrooms alone, surfing the Web, watching TV, and listening to music than to come out and face the world. Their parents leave their meals outside their bedroom doors. Some adult *hikikomori* emerge now and then to buy food but spend most of their time in one small room. The *New York Times* reported on one *hikikomori*:

> After years of being bullied at school and having no friends, Y.S., who asked to be identified by his initials, retreated to his room at age 14, and proceeded to watch TV, surf the Internet, and build model cars—for 13 years. When he finally left his room one April afternoon last year, he had spent half of his life as a shut-in.[1]

His case was extreme but not unusual.

> A leading psychiatrist claims that one million Japanese are hikikomori, which, if true, translates into roughly 1 percent of the population. Even other experts' more conservative estimates, ranging between 100,000 and 320,000 sufferers, are alarming, given how dire the consequences may be. As a hikikomori ages, the odds that he'll re-enter the world decline. Indeed, some experts predict that most hikikomori who are withdrawn for a year or more may never fully recover. [2]

All Japan's wealth and prestige can't keep its young men from withdrawing from society and locking themselves in their rooms. For good. And perhaps because of Japan's wealth and prestige, its young women fall victim to another tragedy—*enjo kosai*, or "compensated dating." Young schoolgirls, age twelve and up, in Japan can "date" older men in return for money, cell phones and electronics, designer clothes, and more. Sometimes the date includes handholding, sometimes fondling, oral sex, and even intercourse.

One young woman who had been dating men for money since the age of fourteen said, "Why not? It's there. There are Japanese men willing to pay good money for nothing more than a tease. I could make huge money and get designer brands just for having dinner at a five-star restaurant and being his date…if they later wanted sex, which in Japan is all about the tease and being unattainable, then that just makes the man invest more money in the relationship."[3]

If you're a dad like me, and reading these words (from someone who started dating for money at age fourteen!) makes your blood boil, consider what the *Asia Times Online* says about the reasoning of these young women:

> *Asahi Shimbun* newspaper found that many girls in the *enjo kosai* trade do so out of spite caused by their own father's

behavior. Many of whom are slavishly devoted to long working hours and spend time drinking at hostess clubs, having extramarital affairs and turning up late and drunk at home. Many of these girls think their fathers have their own kogals [dates] for *enjo kosai*, so why shouldn't they reap some reward from the practice?[4]

Dysfunctional dads lead to dysfunctional daughters. The drive to have the best designer clothes and the latest electronic technology leads young girls to become prostitutes.

The other difficult thing for us as westerners to understand is that Japan's age of consent for sexual relations is the lowest of any in the world: in some areas of the country it's just thirteen. And there's no such thing as "statutory rape." If a teenage girl says yes, then a grown man won't be prosecuted for engaging in sexual relations with her. Sadly, *Asia Times Online* reveals "a Tokyo survey by *Friday* magazine found that an astonishing 75% of schoolgirls reported that they had been solicited by older [men] seeking an *enjo kosai* relationship."[5]

The problem isn't just with the girls who date for money, but it's also with the grown men who are willing to pay to abuse them. But modern Japanese society seems to encourage this. If you've ever ridden on a commuter train in Tokyo, you've seen the adult men paging through pornographic "manga" books: comic books that sexualize the innocence of young girls with outlandishly illustrated cartoon teenyboppers. Is it a holdover of the geisha past? Perhaps. What we can know for sure is that God's plan for little girls in Japan does not include being propositioned by grown men and selling themselves for cell phones and designer clothes.

Considering *hikikomori* and *enjo kosai* and what drives wealthy first world young people to these extremes, is it any wonder Japan also has one of the highest suicide rates in the world? In March of 2011 the *Huffington Post* reported:

Japan has long battled a high suicide rate. At 24.4 suicides per 100,000 people, the country ranked second in
2009 among the Group of Eight leading industrialized
nations after Russia's 30.1, according to the World Health
Organization. The Japanese report didn't calculate the
2010 suicide rate, but its statistics combined with last year's
population report indicate it would be 25 per 100,000.[6]

Japan's next generation is not, perhaps, in need of what we
would think of as "social justice." (Although, after the earthquake-
tsunami-nuclear disaster, many hundreds of thousands actually
were in need of basic necessities.) But clearly, in this wealthy, industrialized nation, something has gone wrong that threatens the next
generation—perhaps not with poverty, not with starvation, not
with violence, but with bitter hopelessness, despair, and a future
that offers no joy. They are shut-in, sexually exploited, and suicidal.

Surely the children and youth of Japan deserve *spiritual justice*
just as much as the hungry children in Africa. Surely the young
people of Japan deserve to know the truth, that Jesus loves them,
wants to heal them, redeem them, and bring them hope for eternity.

It's all part of spiritual justice. It's all part of *evangelism.*

Like everyone else, I was shocked by the tragic news of the 2011
earthquake-tsunami-disaster in Japan and the resulting nuclear
threat. But I was also greatly heartened and deeply proud of the
believers there who immediately began to minister to the victims,
not just with God's Word, although we did provide that, but also
with food, clean drinking water, and shelter. They didn't give up
either. I'm thinking of one church team that was going through a
decimated neighborhood, helping people try to clean up or rebuild
weeks after the tsunami. At one home they found a man by himself trying to salvage what he could from his house, which had
been flooded and was still filthy, muddy, and mildewed. He told
them his wife and daughter were still at the shelter, where they had

lived since the earthquake. When they told him that they wanted to help him clean up, tears came to his eyes.

In Japan it's just not that common for strangers to offer help. He was amazed.

Hours later when they'd worked through the worst of the sludge and put the damaged house in some semblance of order, the team leader explained that they were Christians and Jesus had commanded His followers to love their neighbors as themselves. They had helped him because they loved him, because Jesus loved him. Then they offered to pray for him.

Only a tiny segment of the Japanese population claims to be Christian. This man had probably never heard a Christian prayer before, but he readily agreed that he could use some prayer. They prayed together, and the team placed into his hands a booklet called *When the Foundations of Life Are Shaken*. It was originally written by a Japanese minister in the 1990s after the devastating earthquake in Kobe, Japan. He graciously allowed us to update and reprint it and add sections from the Psalms to let people know that even if they don't know Jesus or understand a personal "God," there is hope and comfort for them in the Scriptures.

A few days later the team saw this same man on his bicycle out on the street, and poking out from the pocket of his backpack they could see *When the Foundations of Life Are Shaken*. He didn't make a dramatic choice to receive Jesus—that would be very rare in Japan—but at least he is still considering the truth found in his book and perhaps sharing it with his wife and daughter. Someone who may never before have known anything at all about Jesus has now experienced the love of Christ through the hands of local believers and has a book to tell him more. It's a start.

For him and for thousands in Japan who have received the *When the Foundations of Life Are Shaken* edition of the *Book of Hope*, this is the beginning of spiritual justice. They have the right to know that Jesus loves them and can transform their life and future. This is one way we can tell them.

Initially our church partners had requested Scripture resources for forty thousand children and young people in 2011. But after the earthquake-tsunami-nuclear disaster, many doors opened for them to reach out to people in need. As of this writing already eight hundred thousand copies of *When the Foundations of Life Are Shaken* have been requested and distributed among survivors of the tragedy. The need is urgent. After the Kobe earthquake, there were many suicides and deaths related to relocation because of the quake. (Community is not Japan's strong suit, and some people who committed suicide after the earthquake weren't found for several days, because no family or friends visited them.) The authorities fear another spike in suicides after the 2011 triple disaster—one reason: those relocated by the nuclear threat are ostracized and isolated in case they might be radioactive. This is devastating for children, and of course, it can lead to depression and suicide among adults as well.

For these lives at risk there's no time to waste in delivering spiritual justice, in the form of compassionate aid and the message of salvation.

GOD'S TRUTH PROJECT

I'm very proud of my daughter Diandra, because she is one of the founders of God's Truth Project, a group advocating for spiritual justice, raising awareness on college campuses in the United States, and showing the next generation of Christian leaders and laymen the true foundation of evangelism. You can see their work online at www.GodsTruthProject.com. It's exciting to see Western believers come to the realization that there's no division between compassion and evangelism, that one is born of the other, and that they're truly building the kingdom when acts of love and charity, proclamation of the truth, and fellowship are all one and the same: evangelism.

Social justice is born of spiritual justice, and it's only achieved when we share the story of redemption with those who have not yet heard it *and* when we model it by our loving actions. That is the other critical facet of the relationship between social justice and spiritual justice, like the one you saw in the last chapter in Dennis's and Tiffany's stories. OneHope invests in providing God's Word through the compassionate hands of *local churches and ministries*. The same church that gave Tiffany her *Book of Hope* also stepped up to help her and her mother and siblings, even before their father chose to follow Jesus. The same church that presented Dennis with the *Book of Hope* is now helping him grow in the faith. The local church and indigenous ministries are the very ones who can best provide both compassionate and spiritual aid to the neediest people.

Spiritual justice, providing the biblical message of purpose and hope, along with the compassionate touch of the Savior, sets the stage for social justice. That's God's truth.

Next I'd like to show you how this worked for us in Florida, right in our own backyard.

Chapter 15

CULTIVATE AVONDALE

I DON'T KNOW IF you commute to work. I do. Thankfully it's a short drive for me from my house to the ministry center in Pompano Beach, Florida. I use my drive time to pray, but on one particular morning the many important tasks ahead of me were intruding into my prayer time. My schedule was jam-packed, and I didn't know how I was going to work it all in.

It was one of those moments when the unseen world broke into my seen reality, because I heard the Holy Spirit say, "Take a right."

Huh? I tried to discern the deep, spiritual meaning of this command. Was the Lord calling for a drastic change in the direction of the OneHope ministry? Or in my personal life? As I struggled to comprehend, I could almost hear the laughter of the Holy Spirit, who whispered, "No, literally. I want you to make a right turn *now*."

It seemed strange, but just a few blocks from my office I found myself sitting at a red light, taking a right turn where I normally would have gone straight. I went down a street I'd never been on before into a neighborhood I'd never seen before. I hadn't realized our office sits adjacent to an urban community of Broward County known as Avondale, a small area of about nine hundred residences with about three thousand people—mostly Hispanic, African American, and a few Anglos. Let me tell you about Avondale. According to the 2008 Ministry Area Profile prepared by the Percept Group, Inc., the lifestyle segment labeled "Struggling

Urban Diversity" makes up more than 61 percent of the population as indicated by the US Census Bureau. This is unusual when you consider that demographically the US population is divided into *fifty lifestyle segments,* and only four are represented in Avondale. The area is also extremely nontraditional because of its very low population of married people and two-parent families.

Here I am, the president of a global ministry delivering a biblical message of purpose and hope to ninety million children and youth each year—am I going to ignore the children in desperate need within half a mile of my office? No. That was the Holy Spirit's message for me that day—the day He told me to take a right. If I truly believe every child deserves spiritual justice, then I have to be concerned with every child, including the children of Avondale. I shared this experience with the OneHope team, and they wholeheartedly agreed. There were children in need just a block from our office where we were affecting destiny for millions all over the world. We would not ignore our neighbors. We committed ourselves, as a ministry, to *take that right turn* into Avondale and affect destiny there too.

Many of the statistics about Avondale are sad, but when we first began our research into the demographics, perhaps the most shocking were the crime rates. It was ranked in the bottom 1 percent of US neighborhoods for safety. There were 776 crimes per square mile, compared with 49.6 nationally (and 91 in the state of Florida). There were 153 violent crimes per 1,000 residents, compared to about 23 nationally. And the chance of becoming a victim of a crime was 1 in 44, compared to the Florida state average of 1 in 126.[1]

There was conflict between Avondale's African American and Latino communities, and conflict between the immigrant populations of different Latin American countries; even conflict between immigrants from various states of Mexico.

Our initial demographic research yielded a "thirty-thousand-foot view" of the community, but where we really started getting community-based challenges and solutions is in what I call the "two-to-five-foot research"—face-to-face with people. We conducted door-to-door surveys to discover the attitudes, beliefs, and behaviors of the Avondale population. A representative sample of people in the community were asked what kind of help families needed in the community. "Jobs" was the top answer. Other concerns were for food, childcare, and education (for children). When people were asked what kind of help children needed, "role models" was the number one answer, with "material goods" a close second. When people were asked what services could most improve their lives, "English classes" was far and away the number one answer. When asked whether they knew or could name the churches in the area, the top answer was, "Don't know the churches."

Clearly this was a neighborhood very much in need of the *spiritual justice* I was preaching across the United States and around the world. I asked the OneHope leadership team to pray and seek God's wisdom for how we could address the needs of this community. Together with our partners at Calvary Chapel Fort Lauderdale and Coral Ridge Presbyterian Church, two wonderful missional churches that are affecting destiny in our area, we embarked on a program called Cultivate. The program was designed to bring lasting change to a community in need. Just as we do with new Scripture-engagement programs, we formulated the outcomes we desired for Avondale in response to the most heartfelt needs of the population:

- Increase quality of life for children and youth (spiritually, emotionally, and physically)
- Reduce crime
- Create social capital within the community

With our church partners (whom we call the "stakeholders" in this process), we formulated outreach events, community service projects, and other activities to achieve the stated goals. Over the course of three years the stakeholders have poured spiritual justice efforts into Avondale in a concerted way. While not every activity has been a huge success, we have seen the beginnings of outcome achievement!

- ESL classes have attracted many immigrant single moms. Their fluency in English will be key to helping them get the jobs they need.

- An interviewing skills workshop helped jobless people prepare for interviews as they looked for work.

- Events and activities have equipped children with back-to-school supplies and backpacks, plus the *Book of Hope* and exposure to *The GodMan* film have helped to introduce them to Jesus Christ.

- Feeding events have provided physical sustenance for hungry families and fostered a sense of community as families and individuals of various backgrounds have come together for meal sharing.

- A health fair provided vaccinations for children, blood pressure and cholesterol checks, HIV testing, breast cancer screening, and much more.

- An after-school program and a women's Bible study have been launched. The after-school program is matching up children with godly mentors to directly meet the need for role models that our survey results called for.

- Adopt-a-Family program has allowed small groups at Coral Ridge Presbyterian Church to reach out to individual families, which has made a great impact.

Some of the families have even begun attending church and bringing their children.

- The Refuge, a halfway house and church sponsored by Calvary Chapel Fort Lauderdale within the Avondale community, has also had great success with regular children's programming.

- For Him Christian Academy was opened to provide a quality Christian education and care for children six weeks through pre-K. Dozens of children from the Avondale community walk through its doors and experience the love of Jesus each day.

The high-profile presence of church members and OneHope volunteers within the community and the great array of services and goods offered to needy families have created the social capital we were looking for, and certainly, by God's grace, we've already helped to increase the quality of life for children and youth. Another exciting proof that we're helping to achieve among the desired outcomes: the crime rate has dropped 26 percent since we launched the Cultivate program for Avondale!

As inspiring as these results are, baby Danielle is even more of an inspiration.

DANIELLE

Rosemary from Mexico was one of those unemployed immigrants we were trying to guide and nurture through the Cultivate program, and she began attending the women's Bible study. One of the volunteers reached out to her and established a caring personal relationship. Rosemary revealed that she was pregnant and planning to have an abortion. She was single, alone, and afraid to try to raise a baby on her own. How could she provide for a child when she could barely provide for herself?

But thanks to her new friend, the support of her Bible study group, and the godly counsel she received, she chose life instead. It's still a struggle for her, but she's learning and growing in God, and her Christian friends are helping her cope and move forward, for her sake and the sake of her child.

Baby Danielle is here today because of Cultivate.

Thank God I took that right turn.

Yes, I believe in spiritual justice for every child. God has burdened my heart, not just for Europe, Russia, Africa, Asia, and Latin America but also for the children and youth of North America. And just as He has put this calling in my heart, He has also called amazing, dedicated people together with the same passion to stand alongside me. I think of our North America Director Blake Silverstrom and the way he took the Word of God into a juvenile detention center to affect destiny for some young men who otherwise were headed down a terrible path.

We'd partnered with the venerable Scripture ministry of Awana for an astounding outreach *inside* the walls of Angola state prison in Louisiana. We'd been privileged to help provide Scripture-engagement resources for the children of inmates, who were also studying along with their sons and daughters on the outside. Blake went to the daylong celebration when the inmates who had completed the study were allowed to have their children come into the prison for a ceremony and a party. Blake's heart was moved. He saw what it means to children to know their dads hadn't forgotten them. But he was also launched on a journey of discovery regarding the justice system in the United States and how many juveniles are actually involved in it. The culture of incarceration impacts every part of American society.

- The United States has 5 percent of the world population and 25 percent of the global prison population.[2]

- One out of every thirty-two Americans is either in prison or on parole.[3]

- An estimated two million juveniles have been arrested.[4]

Blake and our North America team saw that here in the United States was another forgotten segment of the next generation in need of spiritual justice. They realized another "right turn" was in order to affect destiny for a very needy segment of the youth population in the United States. They went to work on a new program, which they tested at a juvenile facility right near the ministry center in South Florida. It was there they met Andrew.

ANDREW

His mother had been looking for love, and Andrew and his little sister got dragged along for the ride. They didn't know their father, and the series of pseudo-stepdads and live-in lovers their mom introduced into their lives was awful. She always seemed to find herself an abusive loser who eventually started beating the children too. More times than they could count, Andrew and his sister were yanked out of bed in the night by their terrified mother who helped them grab what they could and then flee to the next town—and eventually to the next bad boyfriend.

Andrew was too young to understand how abnormal this was. He tried to step up to comfort his mother and help parent his little sister. But he was a child too, and this harrowing way of life took its toll. He'd never stayed in one place long enough to make any real friends or get settled into the routine of school. He'd never seen how normal relationships work, and he'd never had a good male role model to show him what it meant to be a man. By the time his mother got a decent job and found a good place for them to live—as a family, without a live-in boyfriend—it was too late for Andrew.

He struggled in school and found himself failing nearly every class. The only friends he seemed able to make were poor students who came from similar backgrounds. It gave Andrew some comfort to know he wasn't the only misfit, and he was soon spending as much time ditching school with these boys as he spent actually attending classes. His new friends introduced him to new ways to forget his troubles. They inhaled spray paint, used methamphetamines, and went to frequent "pharming" parties where everyone brings whatever prescription pills they can find, mixes them all together, and takes a handful.

Of course, prescription drugs aren't free or accessible. When the teens couldn't steal them from their family members, they broke into other people's houses to steal drugs or steal goods to sell for drugs. Andrew was one of the few boys in this motley crew who actually had a driver's license, so he was appointed to drive the getaway car during one of these break-ins. That was the night they got caught.

From the point of view of the juvenile justice system, it was his first offense, and he received a year's probation. But two more arrests, one for aiding in the robbery of a convenience store and another for trying to fill a bogus prescription, rapidly landed him in a juvenile detention center. He was only sixteen years old, with three convictions and facing two years behind bars. And he was addicted to meth. These facts were hard enough for him to face, but then his mother and sister were there in court for his sentencing. Andrew could barely lift his head to look at them. They had depended on him. He had helped to raise his little sister. He had tried to be his mother's comfort and protector. Now he had hurt them, let them down, and disappointed them.

It felt like the lowest moment of his life. But it wasn't.

The state sentenced him to two years with at least one year to be served in a lockdown substance abuse facility for juveniles. This is where Andrew decided his life wasn't worth living. He was sick in his body because of withdrawal, sick in his soul because of the mess he'd made of his life, and sick in his mind because of the hard life he'd already led in his sixteen short years. He constantly made trouble for himself at the center and was disciplined for bad behavior practically every week. The only thing that brought him any relief at all was the thought of suicide, which became a kind of obsession. How would he be able to kill himself here in lockdown? Could it be done? He began to spend hours each day meticulously planning how to end his own life.

But then, one October day, some visitors came to the center—and kept coming, twice a week, speaking to the boys about feelings and choices. They shared thought-provoking videos on DVD and tried to engage Andrew and the others in conversation about character and responsibility. At first Andrew pretended not to be interested. He didn't want to get drawn in—until one of the speakers began to share his own life story, and it was remarkably similar to Andrew's. He talked about growing up fatherless, failing in school, and getting caught up in addiction and crime. He said that he still struggled, but now he had hope for a better future. And he offered each of the boys the *Book of Hope*. He asked them to read it, discuss it, and be prepared to tell him what they thought about it when he returned.

Andrew took it, but when he saw it was about Jesus, he tossed it aside. He'd been raised more or less Catholic, and he knew he was far beyond any hope the Bible had to offer. He was surprised when several of the other boys actually began reading the book and discussing the questions in it and even continuing the discussion when their visitors weren't there. He laughed at them at first. Didn't they know they were too far gone for any religion to save them? Still, their conversations were quite deep, challenging, and yet comforting too. Some of these tough guys prayed together and even cried! And in the meantime, the visitors kept coming, every Tuesday and Thursday, like clockwork. They continued to talk about life choices, responsibility, character, and new life in Christ. They actually seemed to care about the misfits in the center, and they left behind DVDs, books, and CDs.

Finally the man who had originally given each boy the *Book of*

Hope and whose early life had been so similar to Andrew's came back. He asked the boys what they thought of what they'd read in the book. In just a few minutes a lively discussion began. Andrew hung back, as he had done at every visit with these "Jesus people," not saying much and trying to look bored when really he couldn't fail to be interested, especially when the man asked who was ready to take the next step and commit their lives to Christ. Andrew watched in amazement as not just one or two guys, but more than half the group came forward to pray!

And then Andrew could never have predicted this. *He* felt the strongest urge himself to go forward. He felt like his heart was leaping out of his chest, demanding he get up and move. But he was determined not to. He realized, sitting there in the back, trying to look bored, that he had put up a wall around his anger and resentment. That's what his pretended "boredom" was—a way to keep all the pain at bay, a way to feel nothing. And he simply would not allow himself to feel what he was feeling now. He stubbornly remained seated.

Yet he continued attending the meetings when their Christian visitors came. And though he never said he wanted to follow Jesus, Andrew began to feel better about his life and more hopeful about his future. The thoughts of suicide began to recede. He started taking some of the actions that the other boys were doing now as part of their regular Bible study. He wrote letters of apology to his mother and sister. He went three weeks without getting into disciplinary trouble!

He even started looking forward to something—Christmastime. Although he would still be in lockdown and allowed no personal visitors, the ministry team was making a party for them. They'd already brought in a strength team, a dance team, and even a gospel rapper to entertain the boys and talk to them about God. Finally in the days immediately before Christmas Andrew knew he had to take that next step and choose to follow Jesus. He thought telling the other boys and their Christian mentors that he had made his decision would be the hardest thing to do, but it came so easy! As he prayed to commit his life to Christ, he felt such a great sense of peace that he actually smiled for the first time in a very long time.

As of this writing Andrew is looking forward to early release for good behavior. He wants to get into a vocational school and learn a trade. He knows he still faces many challenges because of his record and background, but now he has new hope for the future, the support of a local church, and the strength of Christ in him. His destiny and the destiny of his friends in the juvey lockup have been affected forever, because Blake and the OneHope team were willing to take that right turn to a place they'd never been before, to discover and help young people they'd never seen before.

Andrew and the other boys at the center were part of our initial testing of a new program designed to touch the lives of young people in the juvenile justice system. Today this program is available for churches across North America who want to be the hands of Jesus Christ extended to young people in detention centers. We call it Decide/Inside, and it's packed with an array of exciting Scripture-engagement tools that draw young people into discussions of good life choices, responsibility, and character, and introduce them to Jesus Christ, the only Savior who can give them strength to begin their lives again.

The program was an amazing success, and we realized that most of it could be reproduced by any local church that has a real heart and commitment to bring hope to young people in juvenile lockup. We've prepared the special editions of the *Book of Hope*, the DVDs, CDs, lesson plans, and the suggestions for each week's visits as a sort of "Juvenile Prison Ministry in a Box" available for churches right now. We've even developed a correspondence version of the program for those who aren't ready or able to send teams into the facility on a regular basis.

Now if you were my neighbor just meeting me and asking, "What do you do?" I could tell you, "I go into juvenile halls and help lead young prisoners to real freedom."

What do you say? Do you hear the Holy Spirit speaking to you right now? I think I do. I think He's saying, "Affect destiny. Take a right."

Will you go where He's leading, to a place you've never been before for the sake of young people who are just waiting to receive the gift of life transformation?

Chapter 16

CHOOSING LIFE

ER PARENTS WERE alcoholics. On the mean streets of Pretoria, South Africa, they panhandled to get money for liquor. And if there was any money left over, they fed their two young daughters. The neglected little girls were finally taken from the irresponsible parents by Social Services and eventually put up for adoption. Monitha and her sister were eventually placed in a real family with loving parents. Monitha noticed right away that her new mother favored her sister, but it was all right, because Monitha's new father seemed to love her very much. The girls both had some problems to work out, considering the way they'd been brought up so far, but it appeared that all would be well for them.

Then, just a few short years later, after a battle with cancer, her father died.

Suddenly the family was plunged into terrible grief and difficult economic circumstances as well. The girls' mother had to scramble to try to provide for them, and of course, Monitha was devastated.

All the healing and hope her dad had instilled in her seemed to slip away as he disappeared from her life. She rapidly spiraled into a destructive lifestyle. Her mother was struggling just to keep food on the table and simply didn't have the time and resources to help Monitha. She ran wild as a teenager. This is a dangerous thing to do in South Africa, where 17.8 percent of the population is HIV-positive or has AIDS.[1] By God's grace Monitha was spared the death sentence of AIDS, but her disruptive behavior landed her at an "alternative" school, the place where the worst students go after being expelled from other schools. She was among the "hopeless cases" at a school where the laundry list of problems included:

- Substance abuse
- Teen pregnancy
- HIV/AIDS
- Learning disabilities
- Behavioral challenges
- Lack of discipline

Monitha herself reflected many of the findings of our Spiritual State of the World's Children research in South Africa, where we found:

- Twenty-six percent say their fathers have died or they do not know their fathers.
- Fifty-nine percent say they wonder if their mothers love them.
- And, tragically, 28 percent have considered suicide.

Monitha was in that last category too. When her father died, she was filled with grief and rage. She tried to mask the pain, but nothing helped. So she decided to kill herself. What reason did she have for living? She was going nowhere and could see no future for herself. She was utterly without hope.

It was about this time that the principal of her school invited teams from local churches and ministries to come and talk to the students. In South Africa all schools teach classes designed to help children develop values and character. (OneHope has developed a great outcome-based program for this class, which many school districts have approved. We've been privileged to train thousands of public schoolteachers to lead these sessions centered on the life of Jesus Christ.)

In Monitha's case the principal of the school was desperate for anything that could turn the students from their self-destructive path, so he agreed to let the teams have the whole school for an entire day of classes. We planned an amazing program that was sure to touch every student with the good news.

Throughout the day various classes moved between the different ministry points, and by God's grace and with all accounts, it was an intensely meaningful time for students and teachers alike. One important part of the program, considering the AIDS rate and the incidence of teen sex in South Africa, was that our volunteers challenged young people to abstain from sex before marriage and avoid contracting sexually transmitted diseases.

Monitha, though, had come to school that day with her mind made up. She wanted to die. She was trying to figure out how to kill herself in a way that wouldn't cause her too much pain. As she shuffled from presentation to presentation, none of it seemed to matter to her. What difference would it make now to develop good study habits? Why worry about AIDS or addiction if she would be dead tomorrow? But as the different groups began to speak of the love of Jesus Christ as an answer to life's problems, some tiny seed of hope began to bloom inside her heart. By the time Monitha saw *The GodMan* film and understood that Jesus had loved her enough to die for her, she was ready to believe that He could be her Savior! By the end of the day Monitha had chosen life and had chosen to follow Jesus Christ.

This decision was a turning point in her young life. She was eighteen years old, what we would call a senior in high school. She'd had no prospects when she came to school that day. She was failing her classes, and even if she had wanted to live, she had no hope for the future. How could she go to college or get a job when she'd made such poor marks in school? But after her encounter with Jesus Christ and after she experienced His life-transforming love, things began to change!

The destructive behaviors began to ebb away. Monitha was reconciled to her mom and sister, and her grades in school began to improve. Her school principal was so impressed with her transformation that he wanted to help her find her way in the workforce. He asked her what she would like to do upon graduation. Monitha's only real career passion was hair and makeup. The principal saw that she was talented and that she now had the determination to succeed, and he offered to pay for her to go to cosmetology school! She could pay the money back once she was established in her work.

Monitha's story is another beautiful example of how spiritual justice brings about social justice, because God is the originator of all justice! Our South Africa team and partners made the decision to affect destiny for a generation, and their faithfulness affected Monitha's destiny for today and for eternity!

VERA

You can see the same pattern in the life of a child named Vera.

She was a little Gypsy girl in Russia. The "Romany," the Gypsies, you may know, are often considered second-class citizens wherever you find them in Eastern Europe—*if* they're considered citizens at all. Vera and her family were no different. They lived in a permanent Gypsy encampment on the outskirts of a city, but they weren't served by any of the civic amenities, and no one watched to make sure the Gypsy children went to school, so they never did. They were pathetically poor. They were considered outcasts, stereotyped as thieves, and Vera's mother's career as a fortune-teller didn't help matters. Vera often felt rejected and alone. Her father was an alcoholic, so there was no comfort there.

The only people who were ever nice to Vera and the other Gypsies were some Christians from a church near their settlement.

They even invited Vera to come to Sunday school. She was so lonely and so starved for human companions who might treat her with respect that she gladly accepted the invitation. She loved being in class with the other Christian children, who were reading through the *Book of Hope* together week by week. Vera even received her own book! Of course she couldn't read it, because she'd never learned how to read. But nevertheless, she liked the illustrations, and the stories she heard discussed at church were delightful to her. She couldn't get enough of this "magical" Jesus.

And now she had friends too—the other Sunday school children!

It's my belief that children and youth are some of the most profound agents for change we can ever reach with the gospel, because their hearts are always open to sharing what they've found. In this case Vera's Sunday school friends were the ones who invited Vera to come to church for a special event, a showing of *The GodMan* film. As she watched the movie, everything became clear to her. All she had heard about Jesus at Sunday school came alive, and she chose to follow Him as Savior.

Vera was so happy to know she was no longer alone. Even if she seemed "invisible," even if people refused to see her because she was just a "Gypsy brat," and even if her father *couldn't* see her through his alcoholic haze, no matter what, she had a friend in Jesus.

And she had her church family too. The other children and adults took an interest in Vera and visited her at the Gypsy camp. Vera, along with her new Christian friends, shared the gospel with her mother, who soon began attending church too. It wasn't long before she gave up fortune-telling and psychic powers and chose to begin a new life with Christ. The church continued to support Vera and her mom and even helped get Vera enrolled in school. How excited she was to learn to read! Now she can read about Jesus for herself in her *Book of Hope*.

Social justice is still a long way off for the Romany of Eastern Europe and the former USSR. But spiritual justice has raised Vera and her mother from poverty and illiteracy to new hope in Jesus Christ. It's love that ultimately makes the difference.

Love for All Humanity
Empowers Spiritual Justice

Good people with good hearts who want to do good things for the suffering may indeed help the less fortunate. The outpouring of donations for disaster relief in response to the appeals of celebrity spokespersons is proof that Christians and non-Christians alike can make a life-saving difference for those in deadly peril. But only one form of aid will make a lasting impact that transforms lives here and now *and* bring hope for eternity. What's the difference? It is love, the love of the Savior, Jesus Christ, as the apostle Paul outlined for us:

> If I speak in the tongues of men or of angels, but do not have love, I am only a resounding gong or a clanging cymbal. If I have the gift of prophecy and can fathom all mysteries and all knowledge, and if I have a faith that can move mountains, but have not love, I am nothing. If I give all I possess to the poor and surrender my body to the flames, but have not love, I gain nothing.
> —1 Corinthians 13:1–3

Love for all humanity, as beings made in the very image of God, is what empowers spiritual justice to bring about social justice. The way the secular world goes about alleviating suffering, in some cases, bears a marked difference from the way followers of Christ approach the same endeavor. There are many examples. The United Nations sent peacekeepers to Cambodia after the fall of the despotic dictator Pol Pot with the highest intentions of helping restore a stable society for the people who had been so horribly terrorized and tortured. But within a few years of the troops' arrival, the number of prostitutes in Phnom Penh had skyrocketed.

The intentions were admirable, but a real love and respect for the Cambodian people weren't foremost in the hearts of every person there to "help." Today Cambodia is one of the global destinations for those who patronize child sex workers.

Or consider the problem of overpopulation in China. The non-Christian solution designed to alleviate the suffering of too many people in too small a space was to prevent more people from entering the world. While theoretically it alleviates suffering by reducing population, forced abortions and infanticide *cause* their own kind of suffering on the helpless babies and their mothers. *Love* for the moms and the babies, for all people made in God's image, would have found a better way. (And indeed some Christian charities allowed to operate in China *have* found that way by rescuing baby girls who are unwanted and providing for them or seeing them placed in loving homes where they *are* wanted.)

Haiti, of course, is another example of how social justice motivated by anything but the love of Christ goes awry. I overheard a missionary who had worked there for ten years say, "The best thing that could happen in Haiti would be for all the aid to leave."

The best thing would be if all the people trying to help just cleared out?

Little Haiti, with just over 10 million people[2] has the second-highest number of NGOs in the world—second only to India, with a population of 1.2 billion.[3,4] And yet nothing gets done! I read a *Los Angeles Times* article that stated that eleven months after the earthquake that killed 230,000, despite the four thousand aid groups, aid had been practically choked out by the government, the small elite class, and the foreign groups themselves. The Haitian people, who have been pushed from camp to camp, all the while being strung along with promises of new schools, hospitals, and housing, came up with a name for the United Nations' forces and members of foreign aid groups: *touris*.[5] Nothing more than tourists.

It's like a twisted nursery rhyme—"all the king's horses and all the king's men couldn't put Humpty Dumpty together again." The fact is that all the NGOs and relief and development agencies in the world can't "fix" Haiti—or solve our planet's systemic issues—because only Jesus can put people's hearts back together again.

Could this be what the apostle Paul was trying to tell us when he said that giving all our goods to feed the poor and even sacrificing our own bodies accomplished nothing if they were done without love? My experience is, yes. Only a life-affirming, love-motivated desire to alleviate suffering *and* bring hope for eternity is the definition of *true* social justice founded on spiritual justice. Jesus told us, "By this all will know that you are My disciples, if you have love for one another" (John 13:35, NKJV).

Does love leave a hungry child to starve? No.

Does love lead a lost soul to stumble blindly toward hell? No.

Does love leave a Gypsy girl illiterate and hopeless? No.

Does love let her follow in her mother's footsteps toward witchcraft and spiritual darkness? No.

Does love let an impoverished teenager take her own life? No.

Does love give her a reason *to live*? Yes. Yes. YES!

Love, personified in Christ, embraces with hands that heal and with sacrifice that saves to the uttermost (Heb. 7:25). When we speak of social justice, of true spiritual justice, we are speaking of the holistic embrace of love.

I applaud the next generation of Christian leaders in the West for their desire to make things right for those who have been denied social justice. When I was forty years old, I saw the hideous miscarriage of social justice in Swaziland that caused me to rethink all I had thought about ministry before and came to this conclusion: holistic ministry that nourishes both body and soul is the only effort worth our time and the only thing that can affect lasting change. If we're going to give our lives to anything, let's not give it to temporary, stopgap measures that will have to be redone by the next generation. Let's invest ourselves in what is eternal.

Ah. It all comes back to my life verse and the idea of the unseen eternal from 2 Corinthians 4:17–18: "For our light and momentary troubles are achieving for us an eternal glory that far outweighs them all. So we fix our eyes not on what is seen, but on what is unseen. For what is seen is temporary, but what is unseen is eternal."

Spiritual justice, it seems, is another way of saying that the "unseen eternal" must—and will—break into this visible world with destiny-changing power. And when it does, it transforms not only the spiritual but the physical as well, which happens anytime we share the Bible's message of hope—no matter how we dress it up and no matter how it's delivered.

So the question is what are you doing to deliver spiritual justice to your world? In what ways are you affecting destiny for the less fortunate in your neighborhood, your broader community, your city, and your world? You can make a difference. You can affect destiny when you allow the creative spark God has placed inside you to shine out as a light in this sin-darkened world. In the next chapter we'll talk about how.

Chapter 17

CREATIVE SPARK

I WAS TALKING TO the creative nucleus of artistic Christian leaders in India just a few days before the Emmy Awards. I was at the Young Creative Leaders Conference. I was thinking about the Emmys and how some little-known or B-list actor would get the "honor" of introducing a two-minute video reel of awards that had been presented *before* the TV broadcast—awards for creative arts. It struck me as strange that on a visual media awards show "creative arts" get such short recognition. It struck me even *more* resoundingly when I heard the ideas of these young Christian leaders of India and saw their drive to incorporate the arts into youth evangelism in such innovative ways.

These people get it. Creativity is one of the world's greatest assets. It's the divine spark with every human being, the image of God that follows after Him in a desire to make something new and beautiful. How can we not get excited about it and want to use it to glorify the One who made *us*?

But the Emmys aren't the only ones who gloss over the importance of creativity. Churches do it too. The very idea of a "creativity conference" like this one would have seemed like a waste of resources to some Christian leaders I know. Why not focus on prayer? Prayer is important. Why not educate people about Sunday school? Children need effective Sunday school programs. Why not a conference to explore discipleship? New believers certainly need to be discipled in their churches. These have historically been the topics and activities the church has invested in. More recently it has been the issue of leadership that has captivated our attention. And in a nation like India, with its fast-exploding population, pervasive poverty, and religious conflicts, is *creativity* really worth a week's time and attention?

I would support a conference on any one of those issues, but I am convinced that in the midst of all these very important subject matters, the church has missed out on perhaps the most powerful element in the cosmos: creativity. The subject of creativity has been overlooked and marginalized to the church's peril. The world has stolen our God-given mandate to use our creativity to influence and transform culture.

It is understandable why the church is uncomfortable in the arena of the creative arts. Scripture tells us that it was the most creative and artistic of the angels, Lucifer, who began the rebellion in heaven against God's authority and supremacy. Lucifer tried, and is still trying, to usurp and pervert one of the most powerful aspects of God's nature: His ability to create. But Lucifer's attempts are just cheap imitations of the true Creator.

God is creative. In the beginning God spoke. For God speaking is action intrinsically tied to the concept of creativity. God said, "Let there be light," and there was light. Out of nothingness God created the heavens and the earth. His creative word established everything. His artistry is in everything we see, hear, and feel. Even we ourselves are a product of His handiwork. And awesome wonder of wonders, He chose to create us in His image. This was the most dangerous of decisions. Even after seeing how Lucifer misused his creative, artistic nature, God still decided to form us into creative beings with the ability to think, develop, and innovate.

When we express our own creativity, we reflect the reality that we are made in the image and likeness of God. And that's why Satan hates it. At every turn the enemy tries to distort or destroy the creative power of God's people. We've seen how the gift of creativity can be used for destruction. Writers and photographers have used their God-given abilities to create pornographic content. Actors have misused their talents to depict violence, perversion, and debauchery. The very talents that God designed to be used to honor His name have been used to blaspheme His name.

But misuses of creativity haven't only happened *outside* the church. We have tragically watched those who once proclaimed Christ fall to the temptations of self-aggrandizement and self-indulgence. The reality is that if God's Word does not govern our hearts and minds, then the enemy twists our creativity, perverts our art, and uses it for evil rather than good.

While the perversions of God-given creative power permeate our culture, I propose to you that Satan's greatest tactic hasn't been to shout us down, but rather to silence us. His most effective weapon has been the subversion of the church's and godly people's ability to use the creative force that God intended for us to use to lift up and redeem all that He made and intended for us.

That's the scary news. But here is the tremendously good news. When we tap into God's creative power within us to speak, proclaim, sing, act, and produce, the power of His Word will transform those trapped in the darkness and despair. In these end times the church must recapture our rightful creativity and relate the gospel story in a fresher, more relevant and dynamic way than ever before.

This was the message I brought to my brothers and sisters at the Young Creative Leaders Conference in India to encourage them in their innovative attempts to affect destiny for the young people of their nation: We must not run away from the battle for our culture; we must run toward it. We must take our God-given ability to innovate, create, and catalyze a movement of creative expression that will capture the hearts and minds of this generation with the truth and beauty of who Jesus is.

The global church is crying out for a creative spirituality that resonates, not through mimicry of the materialistic majority but stands opposed to it by the power of true spiritual enlightenment. I know this, because I have seen it through the ministry of OneHope, again and again.

I can't give you many details because of security issues, but in one majority Muslim nation of the Middle East, churches have really rallied together as our ministry partners to support a summer camp-style creative arts program and festival allowing young people to study, practice, and produce their own works of art based around biblical themes.

The very first year a teenaged girl who had signed up to take part in filmmaking as a writer told the leadership team that she now would rather be a producer. Because they had carefully planned each segment of the program, they asked her to stick with writing because that's where they had planned for her to be and they didn't have another writer to take over if she moved to producing instead. At first Sarah was having difficulty with the task. Her father had recently died, and she was dealing with the grief of his death. The writing did not come easily. But as she worked together through the camp activities and helped her team come up with their film concept, things began to change for her. Through writing her team's script and studying the Bible story that was the genesis of their film, she began to feel comfort after her father's loss. She began to feel hope again!

Sarah won the camp award for Best Writing, and her team's film won Best Concept. After all the films were reviewed, a Christian satellite TV station even asked Sarah to consider writing the script for a pilot television program to air throughout the region. Today Sarah, now a sixteen-year-old young woman who lives in the southern part of her country, continues to help lead the creative arts summer camp and has also had the opportunity to write some scripts for a pilot project.

That first year we had 12 churches participating, with 108 students like Sarah involved. The second year of the program we had 72 churches participating and about 1,800 young people involved.

The following year 110 churches sponsored the event, and 2,500 young people took part. It just keeps growing, because young people are attracted to filmmaking and the arts—and because young people in this region desire to express themselves through media and technology.

During the turmoil in the Middle East in 2011 this concept was expanded. Our research in a particular area showed a general lack of understanding on the topic of forgiveness. Our ministry partners developed a six-week filmmaking curriculum for high schoolers that included a study of Matthew 18 and the parable of the unforgiving servant. In the initial program the class was divided into two teams and given the goal of producing a short film that presented a modern version of the parable. A Facebook page was created to feature both videos, and students at school could join the page, watch the videos, and vote on the one they thought was better. The goal was to see at least 200 students registered for the Facebook page by the end of the two-week voting period. By the end of the *first day*, 225 students had already joined the site! As of this writing the program has now been refined and rolled out in twelve more high schools. We may not be reaching millions of students, but in a region where Christianity is the minority religion and conflict has been raging or is barely controlled, these programs are truly a God-given miracle.

This idea of engaging young people in the creative arts as we present God's Word to them has opened a wonderful door to reach the next generation with the gospel. It has also helped empower Christian young people actively pursuing excellence in the arts with a means to reach their peers. I believe this may represent one of the most important and most powerful venues for affecting destiny in our time. This is why OneHope is at the forefront of catalyzing a movement among Christian young people to impact and transform their culture. The power of art to affect destiny will build faith in young believers and draw their peers to the beauty and love of Christ.

Mateo

Brent Ryan Green and Jeff Goldberg are the cofounders of Toy Gun Films. Their powerful, high-quality short films are making a dramatic impact, presenting God's Word in an innovative way to specific target audiences.

For instance, their film made a tremendous difference to a boy named Mateo. He might have been considered a typical Colombian teen. He had been "jumped" into a gang—that is, given a "friendly" beating by his new gang brothers to prove he was tough enough. He had quickly become one of the gang's instigators of crime and violence, helping to lead his brothers in jacking cars and robbing people on buses, all to get money for drugs. He, of course, used drugs himself; he found release from the constant pain in his heart and mind by tripping on hallucinogens.

He was sixteen years old.

Our research shows that 24 percent, nearly one-quarter of Colombia's children and youth, say they've had suicidal thoughts—and no wonder, considering the culture of lawlessness and violence that pervades the nation and the common experience of broken homes and dysfunctional families among so many children.

Mateo was a product of this environment. His father had been abusive and then absent. He deserted the family, and Mateo's mother struggled to provide for them working as a domestic ser-vant. She couldn't control her adolescent son, who practically quit going to school. When he did go, he was often high. His grades were terrible, but he didn't care. School wasn't going to help him in his life of crime. The way to be successful was to make it to the top of the gang, then to make your gang the top one in the city. Fighting, stealing, drinking, and drugging—these were Mateo's daily pursuits.

But then one amazing day he saw a movie that changed his life. What was the film? *En Tus Manos,* which means "In Your Hands."

Because we are an outcome-based ministry, the genesis of our new programs and products is usually in market research—talking to our target audience, listening to the voice of the young people, asking them what will meet their needs. What we have found, almost universally, is that young people are drawn to the media. They want to watch movies.

Our research also made it clear that huge segments of the youth population in Latin America were being devastated by domestic violence, alcoholism, and drugs just as Mateo was. The innovative cofounders of Toy Gun Films took the research, discovered an amazing true story of how God's Word made a dramatic difference in those very bleak circumstances, and created a short film that speaks directly to the hearts of impoverished children in Latin America.

En Tus Manos tells the true story of a Colombian boy who wants to be an artist but is abused by his drunken father and pressured by his friends to join a gang. At his breaking point, he, like Mateo, is jumped into the gang and given his first assignment: to kill a pastor whose good works are interfering with the drug trade in the neighborhood. This beautifully told story is a gripping testimony to the power of love and the power of God's Word to transform.

By God's grace this hard-hitting film has now been seen by more than 1.4 million young people in northern Mexico, making it *the most watched film in Mexico.* And more than 600,000 young people have seen it in Colombia, where seven thousand partner churches have embraced the film. It is also making an impact in Hispanic communities in North America and other nations of Latin America.

"I cried the entire time I was watching *En Tus Manos,*" one Colombian pastor said. "I was feeling the pain of the youth in my community and the urgency to minister to them immediately, because sometimes they think they don't have hope. But we know that they do. This film is an opportunity to share the gospel with them."

The results of the film showings have been astounding, as so many boys and young men identify with the difficult choices faced by the boy in the film and want to leave their gangs. When Mateo saw the film, presented by a local church, he experienced a visceral connection to the lead character and his dilemma.

"When I saw the film, I just felt like crying, and I didn't understand why," Mateo says. "I was taking drugs and spending most of the time with a gang. I understood that if I continued down that path, I had no future."

After the film showing, the pastor explained how to move in a new direction by walking with Jesus Christ. Mateo felt compelled to pursue this new life with Christ. Mateo ran to the pastor and told her, "I don't want to live this gang life anymore."

"Only Jesus can change you," she replied and led Mateo in a prayer to receive Christ as Savior. From that moment Mateo dropped out of the gang, got off the drugs, and began serving Jesus.

God opened the door for Mateo and his family to move to another city, where he has joined a local church and continues to grow in his faith. Now and then he calls Pastor Anne, back in his hometown, just to thank her for showing that film in his old neighborhood and for giving him the chance to find Jesus as Savior.

En Tus Manos is a wonderful example of a new way to present a biblical message of purpose and hope to a specific target audience: young people who are victims of broken homes, child abuse, alcoholic parents, and poverty. These young people might not be inclined to read the Bible, but when they experience *En Tus Manos* and see how the Word of God makes the difference for the boy in the film, their hearts open to the gospel. And *En Tus Manos* is not the only short film our partners are using to address the heartfelt needs and issues of the next generation.

As I write this, churches in Japan are addressing the issue of *enjo kosai* (compensated dating, discussed in a previous chapter) through the film *Paper Flower*. This is a beautifully produced film, very much in the spirit and culture of Japan; it was also created by Toy Gun Films. The film touches on the high incidence of suicide among Japanese young people. Churches use the film with a curriculum that helps bring these sensitive subjects to light in an authentic, transparent discussion with young people. We've discovered that a film like this can speak more eloquently to the human condition and really confront young people with the truth of God's Word in a way that slips past their barriers and opens their hearts to the dialogue.

Certainly this has been true with *En Tus Manos,* and we believe it will be the same for *Paper Flower.* By the time you read this, we may well have completed the third film made by Toy Gun, which shares the story of an African child soldier, like Dennis, whom you met in a previous chapter. These films are simply innovative ways to introduce a biblical message of purpose and hope to boys and girls, and to young adults, who might otherwise never enter a church or read a Bible. For churches bold and committed enough to use them and open themselves to frank discussion of the issues, these films, by God's grace, provide the catalyst for life transformation.

Films, music, literature, and art can connect with young people at a soul level in ways that preaching can't.

This mission of connecting God's Word to young people in a relevant way, at their point of need, *is* what it means to affect destiny. It's our mission and calling. I believe it is *your* mission and calling too. Wherever you are and however God has equipped you, I believe you too have a creative spark of God's divine nature waiting to be unveiled. I pray you will discover it and use it for His glory and to affect destiny for those who have yet to know Him.

Conclusion

PRESCRIPTION FOR SUCCESS

M Y WIFE AND I have issues. One of them is driving. My wife doesn't understand that God has given me a supernatural gift enabling me to drive at very high speeds with skill and acumen unknown to most humans on the planet. She doesn't get this, so my driving is an issue. Another issue we have is drugs. I love drugs. I spend half my life on airplanes, and invariably the person in the seat next to me for a nine-hour flight is hacking up their lungs from some highly communicable respiratory disease. By the time we hit the ground, I'm already feeling a tickle in my throat, and my next stop is the doctor's office for some drug that will cure me.

Doctors do what they have to do. They ask you questions about your symptoms, take your temperature, monitor your blood pressure, draw blood, listen to your heart. By the time my doctor does all this, if she sits down to give me her opinion and isn't simultaneously pulling out that little white pad to write out a prescription, I get nervous. If she tells me it's just exhaustion and I need to rest, it doesn't make me very happy. I don't want to rest. I want the pill, the preventative, the prescription.

My wife doesn't feel this way. She would rather not take drugs. She is into holistic medicine. She found a holistic doctor who feels the same way she does. They want me to drink more tea and do strange things to my colon. "I have a sore throat. I don't think this is going to help me." This isn't what I want. I want the prescription, I want to take the pill and feel better.

This is why I love Ephesians chapter 1. In this chapter the apostle Paul gives a very clear directive, a prescription for purpose to the Ephesian church. He spells out for the believers exactly what will give significance and meaning to their lives. Within some of Paul's letters you can tell he's exasperated with the people he is writing to. ("Oh you foolish Galatians!") But he founded the church at Ephesus, and you can tell that he loves these people and thinks of them with a father's heart. He loves them so much and wants so much for their lives to have eternal purpose and meaning that in about verse 15 he actually begins to pray this prescription for purpose over them.

> For this reason, ever since I heard about your faith in the Lord Jesus and your love for all the saints, I have not stopped giving thanks for you, remembering you in my prayers. I keep asking that the God of our Lord Jesus Christ, the glorious Father, may give you the Spirit of wisdom and revelation, so that you may know him better. I pray also that the eyes of your heart may be enlightened in order that you may know the hope to which he has called you, the riches of his glorious inheritance in the saints, and his incomparably great power for us who believe. That power is like the working of his mighty strength, which he exerted in Christ when he raised him from the dead and seated him at his right hand in the heavenly realms...
>
> —EPHESIANS 1:15–20, NIV

He wants the church he loves to walk in a spirit of wisdom and revelation. Throughout the Bible as you read the stories of great men and women of God, you can see this spirit of wisdom and revelation at work. When the prophets and apostles were operating in this spirit, God was constantly doing great things through them!

I hope you have seen throughout my story here, that in my life as I've waited upon the Lord and drawn closer to Jesus, this spirit of wisdom and revelation has broken into my world too. There's no other way to explain things like the Holy Spirit's direction to go to Kemerovo, Russia. We were able to impact the city and the surrounding unreached people groups. (By God's grace we planted three churches that still thrive to this day and saw thirty thousand people come to Jesus Christ after one amazing outreach!)

In Paul's earnest prayer for the Ephesians—that they will walk in the spirit of wisdom—he asks for this in the name of Christ, specifically so that the believers will know Jesus better. This spirit is only imparted by Christ, to draw people to Christ. If you want to walk in wisdom and revelation, you must want to know Jesus better. And that's a dangerous thing. At the beginning of 2011 I prayed, "Lord, I know You can do anything, and I want to know You better." With this prayer began the eventful year in which I battled virulent E. coli, which I picked up in Central African Republic. And in the middle of the aggressive treatment, as I lay in the hospital, the doctor arrived with more good news—they'd discovered I had cancer. Once the E. coli was brought under control, I had to endure treatment and surgery for cancer. About five months of the year I was more or less completely incapacitated by illness. It was the worst year I could remember in a long, long while.

Yet, in many ways, it was also the best.

Throughout this year of pain and humiliation (believe me, the symptoms of E. coli are nothing if not humiliating) I drew closer to Christ than ever before. When all other comforts are taken away, we fall back on Jesus and discover He is enough. In fact, He's more than enough. I had prayed to know Him better, and He had given me five terrible, beautiful months when I couldn't work or play, but I could pray and listen for His voice. The wisdom and revelation He poured into me in those months are gifts I would not trade, for anything.

(I want to thank everyone who prayed for me; I don't mean to imply I was comfortless in those months. I could feel the prayers and loving support of my wonderful wife, my family, my coworkers at OneHope, my friends around the world, and the churches that partner with us. Those prayers helped to carry and sustain me. They were another gift revealed in my suffering.)

When we pray, as the apostle Paul did, for wisdom and revelation, we cannot be too picky about how Jesus imparts it. Even if it is through suffering, believe me, it will be worth it.

There's more to Paul's prayer. He prays that the hearts of his friends will be enlightened—that their eyes will be opened—to the glorious inheritance that is theirs in Jesus. We know that our inheritance is that of redemption and salvation, but there is so much more. I think this is what Paul is saying. He wants God to open our eyes to the fact that not only are we saved and redeemed, but also we've been given citizenship in God's kingdom. We're citizens of Zion, of the New Jerusalem, of Christ's kingdom, which is not of this world. Paul wants our eyes to be opened to the rights and benefits of the citizenship we enjoy, and he wants us to understand that with these rights of citizenship, there also come great responsibilities. What is the obligation of the citizens of God's country? To extend the kingdom, to share the gospel, and to invite others to join us.

I fear that too many believers have become focused on their earthly kingdom and forgotten their true citizenship. They work hard to build something they can pass on to their children and grandchildren, but it is something that belongs to this world, which is passing, rather than something eternal. We want to pass on an earthly inheritance to our descendants, something that we can see and touch, because our eyes haven't been opened to the unseen world and our true, eternal inheritance. Paul prays that our eyes will be opened.

This is one reason I can bless my year of struggle and trial. When your health is gone and you're forced to face the fact of your own mortality, it's an eye-opener. You begin to see that any money, any property, any business you might invest yourself in building up to leave as a legacy, is not nearly as important as what lies beyond this world we see and touch. The unseen world breaks into our world when we suffer and assures us that this life is so much more than what we see. My eyes were opened in so many ways, just as Paul prayed they would be.

Then, after praying for our spirit of wisdom and revelation and for the opening of our spiritual eyes, Paul prays that God will show us "his incomparably great power for us who believe. That power is like the working of his mighty strength, which he exerted in Christ when he raised him from the dead" (Eph. 1:19–20). He is saying this power is available to us here and now—the same power that raised Christ from the dead! This power, available to you today, is greater than any obstacle you may be facing, greater than any other power or dominion on earth. We forget so easily who we are in Christ and what power is ours in His name. No wonder Paul prays so earnestly that we will know this power. Think what it can do!

Jesus was dead and buried. It looked to all the world as if His plan and His purpose were finished. His disciples were mourning. Satan was rejoicing. All the hopes and dreams of those who thought Jesus was the Messiah were dead. Then this power of the Holy Spirit raised Him up and brought Him forth from the grave triumphant. The veil that separated man and God was torn asunder. The hegemony of evil on earth was broken—Jesus had seized the keys to death and hell, and all things were made new. This is resurrection power—to revive and renew that moribund dream that you've set on the shelf and forgotten. What would we do if we really believed this power was available to us?

The stories I've shared in this book have demonstrated this power over and over again in my life and in the work of OneHope. Our plan is so outrageous, our vision so audacious, we couldn't move another step forward if it weren't for the resurrection power at work every moment. God's Word for every child and youth on earth? Impossible! Just as impossible as the idea that a crucified and stone-cold dead Savior could rise again and ascend to heaven…but it happened. God raised Him up, and now, Paul says, He has "seated him at his right hand in the heavenly realms."

God can meet you where you are, even if it seems to be the darkness of a tomb, and raise you up. The apostle Paul prayed this over his friends in Ephesus, and the Scriptures tell us that a great cloud of witnesses together with him are praying still for us today (Heb. 12:1). Even more importantly, our captain, Jesus Christ Himself, is praying for His children. According to Hebrews 7:25, "He lives forever to intercede with God on their behalf" (NLT). He and the saints are praying that we will begin to walk in the spirit of wisdom and revelation so we will grow close to Christ, that our spiritual eyes will be open to comprehend our true inheritance in Him, and that we'll come to know the power that is ours in Him—the same power that raised Him from the dead.

When these three things have been in operation in my life—and those times have happened, and happen more and more frequently the closer I draw to Jesus—there's always an explosion of the miraculous. You've read about so many of these times in this book, but I don't want you only to take my word for it. I want you to experience it for yourself. This is Paul's prescription for purpose, for meaning and significance. I want you to take this "pill" yourself.

You don't have to be a spiritual superman for this "drug" to work. Spiritual supermen don't need this prescription. It's the sick who need a physician. If you think you're too sick, too weak, too broken, too wounded, too old, too young, too stressed out, or too messed up, then you're exactly the one who needs this prescription—because you're exactly the one God is looking for. Superman can rely on his own power, but sick, tired, and hungry people like you and me have to rely on God. I could almost hear His voice, as I lay suffering with the fever and agonizing symptoms of E. coli:

"I have you right where I want you now. Here, where you can't rely on yourself, is where you can begin to let My spirit of wisdom and revelation carry you, where your spiritual eyes can be opened, and you can begin to feel the resurrection power raise you up."

Is He saying the same to you? Are you listening?

My purpose, I know, is to give God's Word to the next generation. What is yours? I'm praying together with Paul that you will walk in the spirit of wisdom and revelation, that your spiritual eyes will be opened to your true inheritance in Christ, and that His resurrection power will raise you up and establish you to live a life of significance—one that leaves a legacy for eternity!

AFTERWORD

WHAT A JOY to read my son's words in these pages and see once again how God is at work in and through him, through his life, and through his ministry. My spirit resonates with the apostle John's words, "I have no greater joy than to hear that my children are walking in the truth" (3 John 4).

I praise God too as I read the amazing stories in this book of the Living Word transforming young lives and bringing hope to a generation. As the founder of OneHope, the ministry that Rob leads today, I am, of course, particularly drawn to and moved by these stories. But you have a story too. If I could wish anything for Rob's book, it would be that it finds its way into the hands of every believer whose story hasn't yet been told, who hasn't yet discovered the part they can play in the coming of the kingdom, who loves and longs to serve God but hasn't really figured out how.

I was fortunate. When I was seven years old, God gave me a vision that started me down the path I was to follow. As only a child does, I had immediate faith that what God had shown me would be accomplished, so I set out to do it. Maybe your path hasn't been so straight. Maybe your road led you to become a mechanic, a lawyer, a nurse, a housewife, a business owner, an accountant, or a caregiver. Maybe you haven't yet figured out how you can affect destiny for your own children or grandchildren, let alone the children of the world. If this book has fallen into your hands, I'm praying it will be the impetus for you to examine how you can affect the destiny not only of your own children or grandchildren but also for your friends, your coworkers, the children and young people in your neighborhood, the drug addicts in rehab, the homeless people downtown. You never know. Your story might be told in the unlikeliest of places.

You don't have to grow up as a missionary kid in Lebanon or France. You don't even have to be a year old in your walk with Christ before you can begin making a difference by sharing the love and compassion of the Savior. All you have to be is willing to respond to God as the prophet Isaiah did: "Here am I. Send me!" (Isa. 6:8). This response has taken me to every continent on the earth—and I know it will take you exactly where God wants you to go for your story to be told.

One last thing to keep in mind. "For nothing is impossible with God" (Luke 1:37). God gave me and my prayer partners a vision to reach every child and youth on the earth with the good news. Back then people said it was impossible. What about the millions who can't read? What about the millions who speak a language for which there's no Bible translation? What about the millions who live in areas inaccessible to the gospel? Yet we've seen the heavenly Father break down barrier after barrier, overcome obstacle after obstacle, to help us present His life-transforming Word to more than 811 million children and youth as of this writing. It is happening because of His love for the children of the world and His determination that each one should have the chance to love Him back.

Impossible? Nothing is impossible. Now the Lord has given us the blueprint, Vision 2030, for partnering with local churches and ministries in systematically sharing the gospel with every child and youth on the earth. I couldn't see how it would happen back in 1987 when the call first came from the Minister of Education in El Salvador, but I believed that somehow it would ultimately happen, because God had called us to do it and He is faithful. He's your God and Father too. What He has called you to do, He will just as faithfully accomplish in your life as well. Don't think for a moment that "impossible" stands between you and the place God is leading you.

If our vision at OneHope has struck a chord with you, and God is leading you to partner with Rob and me in reaching the next generation with the Word, we welcome your partnership!

Wherever He calls you, don't be afraid to follow and obey. The Lord of the harvest will direct your footsteps and make you one who affects destiny for others. By His grace your story, like Rob's, like mine, will ultimately glorify Him and bring the hope of Jesus Christ to the world!

—BOB HOSKINS
APRIL 24, 2012

NOTES

INTRODUCTION
A WASTED LIFE

1. "Meant to Live" by Jon Foreman and Tim Foreman. Copyright © 2002. Meadowgreen Music Company. Permission requested.

CHAPTER 2
HOW IMPORTANT ARE THEY?

1. 4/14 Movement, *4/14 Window News*, October 2009, http://4to14window.com/newsletter/volumn01/issue10 (accessed May 29, 2012).
2. World Vision, "Advocacy Talking Points: Peace in Northern Uganda," http://www.worldvision.org/resources.nsf/main/talking_points/$file/uganda_talkingpoints_200803.pdf?open&lid=uganda_talkingpoints_pdf&lpos=rgt_txt_download (accessed July 10, 2012).
3. UNICEF, "Factsheet: Child Soldiers" http://www.unicef.org/emerg/files/childsoldiers.pdf (accessed July 10, 2012).
4. Trafficking in Persons Report, 2007, State Department, http://www.state.gov/documents/organization/82902.pdf (accessed May 29, 2012).
5. Trafficking in Persons Report, 2010, State Department, http://www.state.gov/documents/organization/142983.pdf (accessed May 29, 2012).
6. Avert.org, "AIDS Orphans," http://www.avert.org/aids-orphans.htm (accessed May 29, 2012).
7. East 4 South, "Development Issues in Sub-Saharan Africa," http://www.east4south.eu/index.php/eu_and_development/4._development_issues_in_sub-saharan_africa (accessed May 29, 2012).
8. Po Bronson and Ashley Merryman, "The Creativity Crisis," *Newsweek*, July 10, 2010, http://www.thedailybeast.com/newsweek/2010/07/10/the-creativity-crisis.html (accessed May 29, 2012).
9. Luis Bush, *Raising Up a New Generation From the 4/14 Window to Transform the World* (Flushing, NY: 4-14 Global Initiative, n.d.).
10. Central Intelligence Agency, *The World Factbook*, https://www.cia.gov/library/publications/the-world-factbook/geos/us.html (accessed May 30, 2012).

11. ChildStats.gov, "America's Children: Key National Indicators of Well-Being, 2011," http://www.childstats.gov/americaschildren/tables/pop3 .asp?popup=true (accessed May 30, 2012).

12. 4/14 Movement, *4/14 Window News*, July 2009, http://4to14window .com/newsletter/volumn01/issue03 (accessed May 30, 2012).

CHAPTER 6
NOW I SEE

1. Kazbek Basayev, "Russians Mark Beslan Anniversary" *USA Today*, September 1, 2006, http://www.usatoday.com/news/world/2006-09-01 -beslan_x.htm (accessed May 30, 2012).

CHAPTER 8
SO WHAT?

1. Baptist Mission of Swaziland, "Profile of the Swazi People." http:// www.swazimissions.org/Info.htm (accessed May 31, 2012).

2. Swaziland Human Development Reports, "HIV/AIDS and Culture," March 2007, http://hdr.undp.org/en/reports/nationalreports/africa/ swaziland/Swaziland_NHDR_2008.pdf (accessed July 10, 2012).

CHAPTER 10
SEEN AND UNSEEN

1. John Bailey, "What Is Contextualization and Is It Biblical?" *Globe Serve Journal of Missions*, January 2008, http://globeservejournalof missions.org/jan2008/stonecontext.pdf (accessed May 31, 2012).

2. Ibid.

CHAPTER 11
A BETTER MOUSETRAP

1. Nicholas D. Kristof, "Zoellick at the World Bank" *The New York Times*, May 31, 2007, http://kristof.blogs.nytimes.com/2007/05/31/ zoellick-at-the-world-bank/ (accessed May 31, 2012).

2. "The 10 Poorest Countries In The World: Oxford University-U.N.", *The Huffington Post*, http://www.huffingtonpost.com/2010/08/03/the-10 -poorest-countries_n_668537.html#s122175&title=10_Sierra_Leone (accessed May 31, 2012).

3. Jason Mandryk, *Operation World* (Downers Grove, IL: InterVarsity Press, 2010).

4. University of Pittsburg, "A Brief Overview of Candomblé and Umbanda," http://www.ucis.pitt.edu/clas/brazil_art&culture/ Candomble/umbanda_intro.html (accessed May 31, 2012).

5. *Canto de Brazil*, Hiller Photo, http://www.hillerphoto.com/brazil/bahia_3.htm (accessed May 31, 2012).
6. University of Pittsburg, "A Brief Overview of Candomblé and Umbanda."

CHAPTER 13
SPIRITUAL JUSTICE

1. John Piper, Third Lausanne Congress for World Evangelization, October 2010, http://tinyurl.com/7qocmvs (accessed May 31, 2012).

CHAPTER 14
AND JUSTICE FOR ALL

1. Maggie Jones, "Shutting Themselves In," *New York Times*, January 15, 2006, http://www.nytimes.com/2006/01/15/magazine/15japanese.html?pagewanted=all (accessed May 31, 2012).
2. Ibid.
3. William Sparrow, "The Young Ones," *Asia Times Online*, May 10, 2008, http://www.atimes.com/atimes/Japan/JE10Dh01.html (accessed May 31, 2012).
4. Ibid.
5. Ibid.
6. Mary Yamaguchi, "Japan Suicide Rate Still Among The World's Highest Due To Low Job Prospects," *Huffington Post*, http://www.huffingtonpost.com/2011/03/04/japan-suicide-rate-still-_n_831430.html (accessed May 31, 2012).

CHAPTER 15
CULTIVATE AVONDALE

1. "Social Capital Statistics," http://s3.amazonaws.com/churchplantmedia-cms/coralridge/social-captial-statistics-101810.pdf (accessed June 1, 2012).
2. *CBS News*, "The Cost of a Nation of Incarceration," http://www.cbsnews.com/8301-3445_162-57418495/the-cost-of-a-nation-of-incarceration/ (accessed June 1, 2012).
3. About.com, US Government Info, "1 Out Of 32 Americans Under Correctional Supervision," http://usgovinfo.about.com/cs/censusstatistic/a/aainjail.htm (accessed June 1, 2012).
4. Office of Juvenile Justice and Delinquency Prevention, Juvenile Offenders and Victims: National Report Series, "Juvenile Arrests 2009," http://www.ojjdp.gov/pubs/236477.pdf (accessed July 10, 2012).

Chapter 16
Choosing Life

1. Central Intelligence Agency, *The World Factbook*, https://www.cia .gov/library/publications/the-world-factbook/geos/sf.html (accessed June 1, 2012).

2. Central Intelligence Agency, *The World Factbook*, https://www.cia .gov/library/publications/the-world-factbook/geos/ha.html (accessed June 1, 2012).

3. Isabeau Doucette, "The Nation: NGOs Have Failed Haiti," NPR, http://www.npr.org/2011/01/13/132884795/the-nation-how-ngos-have -failed-haiti (accessed June 1, 2012).

4. Central Intelligence Agency, *The World Factbook*, https://www.cia .gov/library/publications/the-world-factbook/geos/in.html (accessed June 1, 2012).

5. Joe Mozingo, "In Haiti, Good Intentions Have Unexpected and Unfortunate Results," *Los Angeles Times*, December 13, 2010, http:// articles.latimes.com/2010/dec/13/world/la-fg-haiti-aid-20101213 (accessed June 1, 2012).

OneHope is an
international ministry
that presents a **biblical message**
of purpose and hope to young
people **around the world.**

This year we will reach over **91 million** children and youth with a message that is **age specific** and **contextualized** based on **research** that we conduct among children and youth, leaders and educators in the countries where we work.

Our **programs** are **designed** to serve **local churches** and **ministries**, so they can help young people **engage** with **Scripture**. We know it works because we **measure** and **evaluate** our programs.

And we do all of this so **lives are transformed.**

For more information about the programs and products you've read about in this book, please visit our website at **www.onehope.net/hopedelivered**

Like us on Facebook
www.facebook.com/affectdestiny

OneHope
GOD'S WORD. EVERY CHILD.

Follow us on **Twitter**
www.twitter.com/followonehope

FREE NEWSLETTERS
TO HELP EMPOWER YOUR LIFE

Why subscribe today?

- ❑ **DELIVERED DIRECTLY TO YOU.** All you have to do is open your inbox and read.

- ❑ **EXCLUSIVE CONTENT.** We cover the news overlooked by the mainstream press.

- ❑ **STAY CURRENT.** Find the latest court rulings, revivals, and cultural trends.

- ❑ **UPDATE OTHERS.** Easy to forward to friends and family with the click of your mouse.

CHOOSE THE E-NEWSLETTER THAT INTERESTS YOU MOST:

- Christian news
- Daily devotionals
- Spiritual empowerment
- And much, much more

SIGN UP AT: **http://freenewsletters.charismamag.com**